Through
Gogol's
Looking Glass

1. Upper left: drawing by V. A. Tropinin (1840-42)
Upper right: drawing by È. Maminov (1852)
Lower left: drawing by K. Mazer (1840)
Lower right: water color by I. Zheren (1836)

Through
Gogol's
Looking Glass:

Reverse Vision, False Focus,
and Precarious Logic

WILLIAM WOODIN ROWE

New York · New York University Press · 1976

Copyright © 1976 by New York University

Library of Congress Catalog Card Number: 75-21982
ISBN: 0-8147-7366-4

Library of Congress Cataloging in Publication Data

Rowe, William Woodin.
   Through Gogol's looking glass.

   Includes bibliographical references and index.
   1. Gogol', Nikolai Vasil'evich, 1809-1852—
Criticism and interpretation. I. Title.
PG3335.Z8R66   891.7′8′309   75-21982
ISBN 0-8147-7366-4

Manufactured in the United States of America

Contents

List of Illustrations

Foreword

This book attempts to characterize Nikolai Gogol's creative vision and to describe and illustrate the world of his creative works. It also seeks to give the English reader at least some idea of the strange experience that awaits one in Gogolian Russian.

Gogol's writing is almost as difficult to translate as poetry. My translations below are intended to show (as much as is possible in English) the effects produced by his unearthly pen in Russian. At times, I purposely retain a strategic word order which seems rather awkward in English. Transliterations in the text stress readability, whereas those in the footnotes are more scholarly.

The focus of this study closely follows the first seven volumes of Gogol's *Complete Collected Works* (Moscow, 1937–52), which contain his creative fiction. The critics whose views have contributed most to my own are Andrei Bely, Vladimir Nabokov, and Carl Proffer. The themes and techniques which I consider most essential, most Gogolian, are generally introduced in Chapter One, discussed in the Conclusion, and traced by the Index. Hopefully my work will demonstrate that despite the great variety in Gogol's written world, many of his themes and techniques remained quite constant.

Whatever his dreams, crises, and flights, Gogol was always Gogol.

I am extremely grateful to Zoya Yurieff for a careful reading of the manuscript and for her numerous vital suggestions. My wife Eleanor also aided me greatly. And I wish to thank Carl Proffer for his insights and encouragement. Of course, I alone am responsible for whatever errors occur in the pages below.

CHAPTER 1

Reverse Vision, False Focus,
and Precarious Logic

Labels comfort us—seductively. Great writers (a label already) tend to resist them. And if this resistance were the sole criterion of greatness, Nikolai Gogol could almost be said to have no peers.

"Romantic," however, is perhaps the most appropriate single term for Gogol's writing. As V. M. Zhirmunsky has observed: "For the Romantic poet art is meaningful only when it in some way crosses the boundary of art and becomes life. The eyes of the usurer coming to life in Gogol's 'The Portrait' show us the maximum tendency of Romantic art." [1] C. M. Bowra has stressed as Romantic the notion that imagination reveals "things to which the ordinary intelligence is blind." [2] Surely these two characteristics (which may be oversimplified as "imagination revealing other realities" and "art becoming life") are prominent features of Gogol's writing.

Yet one almost immediately feels a need to qualify any label imposed upon Gogol. Dmitri Chizhevsky terms him an "ideological romanticist" who founded the Natural School "without really intending to." [3] Donald Fanger observes that Gogol's work "offers a brilliant and highly original combination of the elements of romanticism and realism"; he considers Gogol, along with Balzac,

1

Dickens, and Dostoevsky, a "romantic realist." [4] C. H. Van
Schooneveld has termed Gogol's protagonists "inverted Romantic
heroes." In his view, "The Overcoat" is "a prime example of an
inverted Romantic story." [5] Helen Muchnic has even seen Gogol as
an "anti-Romantic" because "he seeks not to reveal, but to hide,
himself in his work." [6] There is also a kinship in Gogol's work with
"attempts to enlarge consciousness through hallucination," which,
as George Steiner has noted, "played a large part in the Romantic
movement." [7] While writing this book, I considered—and rejected
—Expanding Romanticism and even Fantasmic Realism. Hopefully, the terms discussed below will be somewhat more specific and
useful.

Near the end of his *Nikolai Gogol,* Vladimir Nabokov declares:
"While trying to convey my attitude towards his art I have not
produced any tangible proofs of its peculiar existence." [8] Andrei
Bely, the Russian symbolist writer and ingenious critic, had this to
say in 1909: "The poor symbolists: critics are still reproaching them
for their 'light-blue sounds'; but can you find in Verlaine, Rimbaud
and Baudelaire images as incredible in their boldness as those of
Gogol? No, you cannot; yet we read Gogol and we do not see, we still
do not see, that there is not a word in our dictionary to name him.
We have not the means of measuring all the possibilities he has
exhausted." [9] Bely then concluded: "We still do not understand
what Gogol is, and although we cannot genuinely see him, Gogol's
creative works—narrowed by our wretched perceptual faculties—are
closer to us than all the Russian writers of the nineteenth century."

The phase "narrowed by our wretched perceptual faculties" aptly
suggests the cause of Bely's awe. Gogol's writing seems to expand. It
superimposes the world we normally perceive and at least one other
"reality." Moreover, the interaction between point of view and what
is viewed (both faintly alien, but masquerading as familiar entities)
uncannily abets this expansion. The reader uneasily senses, in Nabokov's words, the "peculiar existence" of what Bely suggests are
unmeasurable possibilities. We are jarred into an awareness of
something oddly stretching beyond the limits of normal conscious
perception. Two unknowns are multiplied by Gogol, yielding fantastic yet teasingly logical results.[10]

Both Nabokov and Bely are of course highly imaginative verbal

2. Sketch by A. M. Remizov

artists. And this is perhaps a great critical advantage. As Zoya Yurieff has suggested, especially in Gogol's case, a writer may write best about a writer.[11] Aleksei Remizov, an extremely imaginative writer, has seen Gogol's works as "a series of wakeless dreams with an awakening in sleep." [12] Concerning Remizov's discussions of Gogol's writing, Yurieff observes: "One must generally become accustomed to the exceedingly expressive, but often cryptographic and paradoxical manner of Remizov in order to glimpse new horizons and old, yet still unfathomed depths." [13] The undeniable truth of this statement raises a somewhat disturbing question: Is Gogol's creative vision so wildly different as to demand a very special reader? Does it take a writer to read best what a writer writes best about Gogol? Perhaps. And yet a rather large audience of readers in Russian have long enjoyed (if that is the right word) the uneasy pleasures that lurk throughout Gogol's world. What follows here is an attempt in English to describe what I feel are three of his world's most distinctive features.

Gogolian reality often seems focused by what could be termed reverse vision. Words are playfully reversed. About to betray someone, a person is typically identified as his "good friend." About to commit adultery, a woman is called a "good wife." Cheating becomes "finesse"; crudeness, "refinement"; and so on. Situations are often the opposite of what they seem. Pleasant, beautiful surfaces conceal evil and danger. A lovely, innocent-looking girl is a vulgar prostitute; a friendly, inquisitive pig may be the devil; a person is really "a devil in human form." As Dmitri Merezhkovsky has put it, the devil's "main power" in Gogol's world is "the ability to seem not what he is." Gogol's two main heroes, he suggests, are both incarnations of eternal, universal evil in the form of human *poshlost'*.[14]

Their fellow characters, we may note, consider Khlestakov and Chichikov to be exceptionally pleasant people. Also, both heroes escape in carriages—Khlestakov's, complete with merrily jingling bell, seems almost to materialize from an idle daydream he has early in the play; Chichikov's seems strangely to blend with, or become a part of, the winged troika which is all Russia. Flight (or escape), especially in dreams (or in the air), is a prominent aspect of Gogolian Romanticism—along with nocturnal gleamings and terrors, upside-down mirror reflections, multiple realities, and a fondness for hyperbole, the grotesque, antithesis and reversals.

"After the Play," Gogol's short dramatic work of 1842, features a lover of the arts who argues that both comedy and tragedy can express the same lofty thoughts. Even the smallest inner crevices of a base and dishonest person's soul, he suggests, "already sketch the image of an honest person" (V:143). He goes on to observe that a skillful physician can treat the same disease with equal success using "both cold and hot water." The work ends with a long speech by the author of the play, who closes on a strikingly similar reversal note: cold laughter can contain hot sparks of love, a strong person can act weakly and a weak one strongly, and, finally, "he who often sheds deep, spiritual tears, it seems, laughs more than all others in the world!" (171).

A character in Gogol's short play *The Ending of "The Government Inspector"* expresses a similar view. Art, he declares, can strive for goodness either positively or negatively. If an author presents all the rottenness a person can contain, so that the spectators feel total revulsion, he argues, is that not already praise for everything good? (IV:125).

All this seems to shed an interesting light on Gogol's famous pronouncement (in "Four Letters to Various Persons Regarding *Dead Souls*") about his own uniqueness as a writer. Quoting Pushkin's opinion, Gogol pointed to his own unique ability to depict *poshlost'* so vividly (VIII:292). We may thus speculate that Gogol (reversely) hoped his uniquely successful painting of *poshlost'* would be seen as an inspiring evocation of goodness and virtue. One thinks of those deceptive silhouette pictures which show either a vase or two faces, depending on whether one concentrates on the blank or shaded areas.

Bely has described the reader's impression of the plot of a Gogolian work as follows. One sits near a mirrorlike body of water, enjoying the clear, precise reflections of clouds, the heavens, trees: "suddenly, some kind of murky spots and shadows, unrelated to the reflection, furrow its contours." In place of the clouds, one sees a school of fish beneath the surface: "fish—in the sky?" [15]

Gogolian narration thus predicates hints of impending revelations. Many such hints become discernible only in retrospect. In this sense, reverse vision seems to affect chronology: the beginning of a Gogolian work typically leans toward its ending.

Due to Gogol's use of ironic foreshadowings, hidden prophecies, and forward-leaning details, many readers are not normally aware of all the factors precipitating them toward the conclusion of a given work. The ending, moreover, typically reveals a reality very different from the one we have been taking for granted throughout. But a closer look, and the alteration is exposed: it was gradually, stealthily occurring all along.

Gogolian reverse vision also gave rise to some rather disturbing psychological, philosophical, and religious questions. Insanity displays an intricate logic even in its wildest fabrications. Dreams are often prophetic. The fantastic seems strangely vivid and real, especially because of its matter-of-fact depiction. God and the devil are constantly mentioned together, as are the devil and women.[16] The devil seems to span two worlds, actively functioning in this one. Often, our casual expressions referring to the devil (and there are very many in Russian) seem to inspire his interference in our lives. Even life and death tend to be reversed: the reader gradually comes to feel that his own world is but a dull, gray prelude to the bright and terrifying next one. And perhaps strangest of all, at least one other "reality" keeps overlapping or showing through in ways which we never quite realize.

V. Zenkovsky has found that Gogol's uniqueness resides in the "multilayeredness" of his works. "Behind the external realism of the tale," he writes, "one continually senses some other, different material which sometimes breaks through in unexpected remarks." [17] Nabokov suggestively stresses "that secret but real world which breaks through Gogol's style." [18]

While suggesting that our firm, solid world is an insidiously deceptive surface, Gogolian narration often utilizes a technique which may be termed "false focus." In many of his reversals, Gogol refers to the dead as living, the imagined as real, the absent as present, and so on. A dead person is repeatedly called "the deceased" as we read of his actions while alive. "Grandfather," in one story, is a vigorous young man. A child wishes to become an ambassador when he grows up: at table, someone wipes "the ambassador's" nose. Seen in a window, a man and his samovar resemble two samovars, except that "one samovar" has a pitch-black beard.

False focus was also used by Gogol in connection with disguises, altered appearances, and dual identities. "Soloha" is really "the witch." "The cossack" is really "the sorcerer," who is really "Katherine's father." "The Government Inspector" is not the Government Inspector, and so on. Gogol repeats a false focus especially often just as the double identity is revealed. For example, a person is repeatedly termed "sister-in-law" while we discover that "mistress" is more appropriate.

Still another manifestation of false focus involves what Carl Proffer has discussed as turning a simile into a metaphor. For example, Korobochka's carriage in *Dead Souls* is likened to a "bulging watermelon placed on wheels." Subsequently, we read about "the watermelon." Proffer observes that the transformation often results from removing the word "as" or "like"—first, something is "like" something else; then, it simply "is" the other thing.[19] In terms of Gogolian reverse vision, the vehicle of the simile has replaced its tenor.

In all Gogol's uses of false focus, the label does not fit the product: the reader must identify it more closely. The technique may seem quite capricious, but it forces the reader to participate in order to clarify what is described. By briefly impeding the reader's perception,[20] false focus thus promotes his vivifying participation.

In Gogol's world, many apparently unrelated details (at least faintly) reflect a far larger picture. Indeed, details are the essence of his writing. "Nothing," finds Bely, "exists without design."[21] Even in widely separated passages, Proffer has demonstrated, Gogol makes use of "interlocking detail."[22] Examined closely, even the most separate, remote elements seem faintly associated. Although with strange or even precarious logic, Gogol subtly interconnects ideas, images, and events.

Gogolian precarious logic ranges in effect from absurd humor to disturbing insight, and it sometimes produces an eerie mixture of both. In a dramatic fragment entitled *The Lawsuit,* Burdyukov suggests that Prolyotov's odd "physiognomy" must be the result of his mother's being terribly scared by something during her pregnancy (V:111). Such things, Burdyukov insists, happen quite often. He goes on to tell of a man whose "entire lower face is sheeplike, so to speak, as if cut off and grown over with wool, just like a sheep. And yet from an insignificant circumstance: when the deceased woman was giving birth, a sheep went up to the window and for some damned reason, bleated." As traced below, Gogol made an especially effective use of such precarious logic by focusing upon human heads in conjunction with the birth of ideas.

Notes

1. V. M. Zhirmunsky, "On Classical and Romantic Poetry," trans. Philip E. Frantz and Ray J. Parrott, Jr., in *Russian Literature Triquarterly*, No. 10, p. 195.

Mario Praz also notes the survival of life in these eyes. *The Romantic Agony*, trans. Angus Davidson (New York, 1960), p. 475.

2. C. M. Bowra, *The Romantic Imagination* (New York, 1961), p. 7.

3. Dmitri Chizhevsky, *History of Nineteenth-Century Russian Literature: Volume II. The Age of Realism*, trans. Richard Noel Porter (Nashville, 1974), p. 19.

Jacques Barzun suggests that Gogol's Naturalism is more closely connected with his Romanticism than with his Realism. *Classic, Romantic and Modern* (New York, 1961), p. 220.

4. Donald Fanger, *Dostoevsky and Romantic Realism: A Study of Dostoevsky in Relation to Balzac, Dickens, and Gogol* (Cambridge, Mass., 1965), p. 101.

Soviet critics are belatedly exploring Gogol's Romanticism. In a recent article, N. L. Stepanov accuses himself and other specialists of having neglected this vital aspect of Gogol's writing. "The Romantic World of Gogol," in *K istorii russkogo romantizma*, Yu. V. Mann, I. G. Neupokoeva, U. P. Fokht, eds. (Moscow, 1973), p. 188. See also in the same volume Yu. V. Mann, "Evolyutsiya gogolevskoj fantastiki" and A. N. Nikolyukin, "K tipologii romanticheskoj povesti."

In a recent (1975) trip to the Soviet Union, I found that Soviet scholars were interested in discussing Gogol's Romanticism. They also quoted (as do the authors of the above articles) opinions on Gogol of various Symbolist and Formalist writers, though sometimes apparently only to disagree.

5. C. H. Van Schooneveld, "Gogol' and the Romantics," in *Slavic Poetics: Essays in Honor of Kiril Taranovsky*, Roman Jakobson, C. H. Van Schooneveld, and Dean S. Worth, eds. (The Hague, 1973), pp. 482, 483.

6. Helen Muchnic, *Russian Writers: Notes and Essays* (New York, 1971), p. 24.

7. George Steiner, *The New Yorker*, February 17, 1975, p. 105.

8. Vladimir Nabokov, *Nikolai Gogol* (New York, 1961), p. 150.

9. Andrej Belyj, *Lug zelyonyj* (New York, 1967), p. 95.

10. Aleksandr Blok has also noted the uneasy, lasting effect upon "one who has looked into the new world of Gogol." *Sobranie sochinenij v vos'mi tomakh* (Leningrad, 1962) V, 377.

V. V. Rozanov speaks of "the strange world of a diseased imagination." *O Gogole* (Letchworth, England, 1970), pp. 28-29.

11. Zoya Yur'eva, "Remizov o Gogole," in *Novyj zhurnal*, No. 51, December, 1957, p. 111.

12. A. M. Remizov, *Ogon' veshchej* (Paris, 1954), p. 28.

13. Yur'eva, p. 111.

14. D. S. Merezhkovskij, *Izbrannye stat'i* (Munich, 1972), pp. 166-167. See also pp. 183, 206.

The untranslatable concept *poshlost'* (to which Nobokov devotes a dozen pages of his book about Gogol) can be suggested as follows: the smug pretentiousness of insidiously self-gratifying self-deception, especially where cultural or aesthetic values are concerned.

15. Andrej Belyj, *Masterstvo Gogolya* (Munich, 1969), p. 43.

As *Hanz Kuechelgarten* opens, "Waves of clouds" are reflected in the "silver water" of the sea (I:61). Later, we see "white waves" made by drowned maidens who swim by moonlight in the same waters (86).

This "idyll in pictures," as it is subtitled, tells a story of mysteriously sad love. Hanz, about to marry his beloved Louiza, is seized by a longing to sample the "agitation" and "excellence" of this world. After two years, he returns to Louiza, and they are about to be married when his former sadness/sickness seems to return.

Characteristically, Gogol ventured into print behind a counterfeit preface (cautiously praising the author's young talent) and the pseudonym V. Alov. Typical also in *Hanz* are the initial father-daughter theme, vivid upside-down reflections, drowned maidens (presumably disappointed in love) who appear by moonlight, a bony, heavily rising corpse, and two prophetic dreams.

In "Picture One," Louiza's father has a delirium-like dream (of her) which mysteriously pierces his soul with a secret sadness and brings on a strange agitation (I:62). Awakening, he mistakenly thinks that the day is foggy (63). After that, both sadness *(toska)* and fog *(tuman)* repeatedly appear at key points. For example, Hanz's gaze becomes "foggy" when his sickness begins (67), and his affliction is later called "not sickness, sadness" (74). As he furtively leaves Louiza, Hanz looks back but a "fog" covers her (81). When she awakens, the "fog" seems to "bring on sadness" (81). The "fog" then leaves (82), but she has an "amazing" dream of "fog" (83). And this dream also becomes prophetic, for although Hanz returns, he is mysteriously "befogged" and lapses into "sadness" as the poem ends (99).

16. As Nabokov has suggested, Gogol seems to have believed more deeply in the devil than in God. Nabokov, p. 73.

17. V. Zen'kovskij, *N. V. Gogol'* (Paris, YMCA-Press), p. 36.

18. Nabokov, p. 143.

19. Carl R. Proffer, *The Simile and Gogol's "Dead Souls"* (The Hague, 1967), p. 83. Proffer notes that Chizhevsky has called the technique "realizing" a simile, and he suggests that it could also be called "metaphorizing" a simile. Also aptly, Proffer speaks of "masterful concretization" (p. 38).

20. The reader's impeded perception, as it relates to defamiliarization or making strange *(ostranenie)*, is discussed below in the section on "Christmas Eve."

21. Belyj, *Masterstvo Gogolya,* p. 44.

22. Proffer, pp. 82, 172.

CHAPTER 2

Evenings on a Farm
Near Dikanka

"PREFACE TO PART ONE"

The theme of *Evenings,* in Gippius's view, is "the intrusion of the demoniac into human life." [1] There are two groups of four stories, each group with a preface, edited by the fictitious beekeeper "Red" Panko.

We learn the editor's profession at once, but Panko reveals his name somewhat later, mentioning what marvelous tales are told

> at the house of the beekeeper "Red" Panko. Just why the villagers have named me "Red" Panko—I swear to God, I cannot say. And my hair, it seems, is now more gray than reddish. (I:104)

In the course of this passage, the reader is led to believe that (1) Panko probably has red hair, (2) he does not, (3) he has only a little red hair remaining. Such syllogistic descriptions are typical, as is the repeated focusing ("Red") on that which is not quite so. [2]
Panko moves on to describe the sacristan of the Dikanka church:

> he will always receive you in loose overalls of fine cloth the color of cold potato mash, for which he paid nearly six rubles a yard in Poltava. From his boots, no one in the entire village

11

would say that the odor of tar emanates; but anyone knows
that he has cleaned them with the very best fat, such, I believe,
as many a peasant would be glad to put into his porridge.
Neither would anyone say that he ever wiped his nose with the
flaps of his overalls, as many people of his calling do. . . .
(104-05)

Gogol sometimes combines food with faint repulsiveness.[3] Here, the
porridge and its buttery seasoning are mentioned in rather odd
conjunction with nose wipings and tar. And the overalls, upon
which the sacristan so vividly does not wipe his nose, have just been
described as "the color of cold potato mash." Indirectly then, even
the potato mash and the nose wipings uneasily reinforce each other.
Later, Panko ends his Preface by inviting the reader to his village for
a feast, so sumptuous that "the butter will run down your lips when
you begin to eat."

The sacristan, Panko informs us, once told a story about a
schoolboy who forgot the name for a garden rake. Asking his father
about it, the boy stepped "with mouth agape" onto the teeth of the
rake. Swinging up, the handle "cracked him on the forehead," and
the boy yelled out: "Damned rake!" (105). Gogol may not have
invented this rather unsubtle joke. However, it is quite typical that
the rake strikes not the boy's gaping mouth, but his forehead. With
what may be termed precarious logic, the rake seems almost to drive
in the knowledge of its own name. Gogol was fond of connecting
ideas with heads in strange ways.

Panko begins his Preface with a beekeeper's apology for turning
writer: "As if enough geese have not been plucked for pens already."
His final invitation to the reader explains that upon reaching Dikanka, one may obtain precise directions from "a small boy in a
dirty shirt tending geese." Gogol was also fond of such faintly
familiar details. In "Shponka," as noted below, the reader is invited
to search for a man who waves his arms like a windmill. Later in the
story, the first thing the hero sees upon arriving home is an oddly
personified windmill.

Notes

1. Vasilij Gippius, *Gogol'* (Leningrad, 1924), p.49. He finds this theme modified in three later stories ("Viy," "Nevsky Prospect," and "The Portrait") as "the intrusion of the demoniac into the beautiful."

2. Also typically, "it seems" *(kazhetsya)* tends to undermine what had "seemed" so before: the redness of Panko's hair. "Nevsky Prospect" is especially rich in this effect.

3. In a dramatic fragment called *The Lackeys' Room*, one character juxtaposes "vodka" and "excrement" twice in a single sentence, once even associating them by referring to the odors of both (V:122).

"THE SOROCHINTSY FAIR"

The surface of this tale incompletely conceals hints of another reality. As Grytsko tricks Solopy and Havronya into letting him marry Paraska, the devil supposedly prowls about in the aspect of an ordinary pig. The trick succeeds, partly because Solopy and his friends are terrified by an ordinary pig. But the ending plants disturbing suggestions in the reader's mind. The entire story seems folded back upon itself, in Gogolian fashion, so that darkness is faintly visible behind daylight, terror behind quiet calm, and an empty, deathly future behind a present that seems brightly, richly alive.

The story begins with lavish praise of nature. We see a reversal: the sky and its "pure mirror—the river in its green, proudly raised frame" (I:112). We then see a man walking along behind his oxen-drawn wagon. Peasants who meet him, especially the young men, reach for their caps. But it was not, we are informed, "his gray moustache and not his impressive step which caused them to do this." Rather, we must raise our eyes slightly to behold "the cause of such deference"—Solopy's pretty daughter Paraska, sitting on the wagon. She has thus been significantly present in the story for several lines before we observe her. An ecstatic description of the girl leads to her "spiteful stepmother," whereupon the narrator interrupts himself: He had "forgotten" that she, too, was on the wagon. The unseen live background is thus double.

"Our travelers" now begin to see the (personified) river, who "had dazzlingly exposed her silvery bosom, onto which luxuriously fell the green tresses of trees. Willful as she is in those rapturous hours, when the faithful mirror so enviously contains her brow full of pride and dazzling splendor . . . and there is no end to her caprices . . ." (113). Even the river background seems strangely alive, as it pictures a proud, beautiful girl. After this, the "mirror" of the river seems to turn everything upside down, whereupon focus shifts back to Paraska.

Near the end of the story, Paraska holds a mirror and dances with proud self-admiration while the entire room turns upside down. Also like the personified river, she seems to enjoy caprices. For

Solopy has been watching, unseen, and now father and daughter begin to dance. They are surprised by the peasant Tsybulya, who has also been watching, unseen.

Still en route to the fair, we meet the handsome lad Grytsko, who loudly praises Paraska's beauty and calls her stepmother Havronya "the devil sitting in front." Enraged, Havronya heaps abuse upon Grytsko, who replies by pelting her new hat with mud (114). The "mud" is later termed "manure" (119).

They arrive at the fair. Paraska notices a lively background of colorful detail, which ends with someone "stroking the beard of a goat." At this point, she feels a pull at her sleeve. It is Grytsko, whose handsome appearance startles and thrills her, yet whose gesture seems oddly anticipated by the final detail in the background picture he interrupts.

While the two young people become affectionate, Solopy learns from another peasant that the fairgrounds are "an accursed place." A pig, it seems, had yesterday thrust its snout out of the window of a nearby barn, grunting ominously. As we later learn, the devil is supposedly roaming about disguised as a pig, searching for fragments of his red jacket. The account of this, which contains numerous terrifying pig snouts in windows, is told at night in Tsybulya's hut, where Solopy and his family are visiting. The story is interrupted by a smashing of window panes: A "terrible pig's mug" intrudes, "rolling its eyes as if to ask: 'What are you doing here, good people?'" (127). This event is presumably contrived by Grytsko and some gypsies to trick Solopy and his wife into allowing Grytsko to marry Paraska.

Since the intruder is believed to be a disguised devil, the greeting "good people" (which is stressed earlier in another context, 125) has a rather ironic ring, especially since Havronya's would-be lover is hiding on the rafters above their heads. Typically, he and she had been interrupted; also typically, he has been an unseen audience for the tale just interrupted. When he now falls crashing to the floor, total panic sets in. Amid cries of "The devil!" Solopy flees, finally falling to the ground, where he faints and lies motionless, "like a terrifying inhabitant of a cramped coffin." (The word "inhabitant" tends to reverse life and death.[1]) Havronya, who also flees, is discovered sitting on top of Solopy. The peasants then jokingly call her the devil, which echoes Grytsko's calling her "the devil sitting in front" earlier. Grytsko has also referred to marriage as "letting oneself be saddled by females" (121). Moreover, just before Havronya sits on Solopy, Tsybulya crawls in terror under his wife's skirt. (The image of a devilish woman atop a man vividly reappears in "Viy.")

Part Six of "Sorochintsy" opens in the evening, with two figures sneaking across a fence. In Solopy's absence, Havronya is leading the priest's son to Tsybulya's hut. At this point she is termed Solopy's "mistress" *(sozhitel'nitsa)*—a typically ironic reversal.[2] Havronya helps the priest's son to climb the fence. Later, when they are interrupted, her suggestion that he climb up and hide on the rafters thus seems faintly anticipated. And his crashing fall from the rafters seems to parallel his noisy fall from the fence into the weeds.

At Tsybulya's hut, the priest's son mentions "offerings," adding that only from Havronya can one receive truly delectable offerings.

> "Here are some offerings for you, Afanasy Ivanovich!" she said, placing wooden bowls on the table and coyly buttoning up her apparently unintentionally unbuttoned blouse, "doughnuts, wheat dumplings, cakes, and buns!" (122) [3]

The words "apparently unintentionally" tend to suggest an intentional display. And of course "offerings" refers rather ironically to food for a priest's son. Moreover, Gogol's focus shifts somewhat playfully to Havronya's revealing blouse before the doughy foods are named. After this, the priest's son declares:

> "my heart craves for foods from you more sweet than all these dumplings and buns."
>
> "Well, I have no idea what other kind of food you might be wanting, Afanasy Ivanovich!" answered the buxom beauty, feigning ignorance.
>
> "Of your love, to be sure, my incomparable Havronya Nikiforovna!" the priest's son pronounced in a whisper, holding a dumpling in one hand and embracing her wide waist with the other.

3. Drawing by V. Makovsky (1875)

Here, Havronya is (reversely) termed "incomparable" just when the Gogolian notion of sexual food [4] becomes most explicit. And if one pictures the priest's son applying himself to the two "doughy foods," the human sexual appetite seems almost disconcertingly humorous.[5]

Gogol's focusing on Havronya's blouse to evoke her body is characteristic. He often views clothes as having nearly organic connection with the person inside. For instance, the physical description of the gypsy who aids Grytsko ends as follows: "all of this seemed to demand a special, in fact, the same sort of costume exactly, that he was wearing" (121). And the gypsy's clothes, we are told, "seemed to have grown on to him and constituted his nature."

Just before Paraska decides to dance with her mirror, she pictures herself married and tries on her stepmother's hat to see how it will suit her. When she dances with her father, Tsybulya interrupts them: "Well, that's fine, the father and daughter have fixed up a wedding here all by themselves!" (135). This "wedding" seems strangely anticipated by the fact that Paraska has just donned the hat of her father's wife. And Paraska's future husband, of whom she thinks while putting on the hat, was the one who hit Havronya's hat with "mud" en route to the fair. Though less obvious, this chain of suggestive details seems not unlike that between rake handle, forehead, and name of rake in the Preface. In both cases, a head comes into focus as an idea is strangely inspired.

The story ostensibly terminates with the festivities of the wedding celebration. "A strange, inexplicable feeling," we read, "would have overcome a spectator. . . . People, across whose sullen faces, it seemed, a smile had not slipped for a century, were tapping their feet and shaking their shoulders. . . . But a still stranger, still more enigmatic feeling would have awakened in the depths of one's soul on seeing the old women, whose decrepit faces emanated the indifference of the grave . . . whom intoxication alone, like the mechanic of a lifeless automaton, forces to perform something humanlike. . . ." The dancers seem like human puppets, from whom the life is persistently drained. But who, one wonders, is the "spectator" of all this? Who sees these live people as deathly, mechanical puppets? "People" are seen as with slightly alien eyes, and the narrator's insights seem strangely vague and uncertain ("it seemed," "humanlike"). We may also wonder about the source of the narrator's frames of reference, his bases for comparison. What special knowledge has he of gravelike emanations; of one's innermost soul; of what, in humans, is humanlike? And why does Gogol select a wedding celebration as the stage for such declarations? Solopy's wife, we recall, was repeatedly likened to the devil; when she tries to stop Paraska's wedding, Solopy thinks of the devil (116). And just before Solopy's wife sits upon him and is likened to the devil, he is compared to "an inhabitant of a cramped coffin," which seems similar to the old women at the wedding party ("the indifference of the grave").

The ending of the wedding celebration seems oddly anticipated by the exclamatory opening of the story.

> How intoxicating, how luxurious is a summer day in Little Russia! How languorously hot are the hours when the midday glitters in the stillness and sultriness, and the light-blue immeasurable ocean, bent like a voluptuous dome above the earth, has, it seems, fallen asleep, completely drowned in comfort, enclosing and pressing the beautiful one in its airy embrace! There is not a cloud in it. In the field not a word. Everything seems to have died. . . . '

The sky-as-ocean anticipates the river as mirror of sky (discussed above). But let us return to the end of the wedding:

> The thundering laughter and songs grew quieter and quieter. The fiddle-bow was dying, growing weak, and losing its unclear sounds in the emptiness of the air. Somewhere, the sound of thudding feet could still be heard, something similar to the hollow rumbling of a distant sea, and everything soon became muffled and empty.

This "distant sea" recalls the initial "ocean" (of the sky). Other details also seem familiar. Before, everything seemed "to have died"; now, the sounds are "dying," and the dancers have just been described as dead puppets, with the atmosphere of the grave. Most significantly, the glorious, "intoxicating" daylight life was earlier transformed into a drowsy death, just as now, "intoxication" gradually fades away, transforming the dancing scene into a silent, muffled emptiness. "Joy," we read, "flies away," and the music "already hears sadness and emptiness in its own echo." The reversal of the ending is thus faintly anticipated by the opening lines of the story.

"The Sorochintsy Fair" richly exemplifies Gogolian reverse vision. For example, it is a priest's son with whom Havronya would copulate, and as her intentions are made clear, she is termed the "mistress" of her husband. Also typically, appearances seem slyly undermined. The pig in the window, we think, is merely a ruse; the folk legend of devil as pig, a mere fabrication. But in the legend, phrases like "devil's gift" seem unsettling in their unwitting truth.[6] Even in the story proper, where the devil and his jacket [7] seem to appear only in people's imaginations, there is a tendency to reverse the worlds of the dead and the living. Solopy is likened to "an inhabitant of a cramped coffin"; the priest's son becomes terrified "as if some kind of emigrant from the other world had just been paying him a visit" (123). The casual, matter-of-fact tone of such observations seem to presume that another "reality" lurks in the background; the narrator has only to notice it. Finally, certain events (Paraska's capricious dancing with the mirror; the priest's son's loud fall from the rafters) seem to have happened before. Even the ending of the story seems strangely similar to its opening, as though the entire tale was folded back upon itself and seen in faintly alien, anticipatory perspective.

Notes

1. A more complete discussion of such reversals may be found in my "Gogolesque Perception-Expanding Reversals in Nabokov," *Slavic Review,* March 1971.

2. While heaping vile abuse upon Grytsko for insulting her, Havronya is called an "elderly beauty" (114). When Solopy reveals he has been drinking somewhat prematurely at the fair, he supposes that Havronya will seize his hair "in her connubial claws" (120). Grytsko's gypsy confederate asks, in obvious triumph, "have we done our job badly?" (133) Typically, these Gogolian reversals do contain a grain of truth. Havronya, even though aspiring to unfaithfulness, is still Solopy's "cohabitant." While anything but a "beauty," she is buxom and presumably quite attractive to the

priest's son. Her "claws" are of course "connubial," and the gypsy's "job," though well executed, does wreak considerable havoc.

3. More technically, "*Varenychky* are curd dumplings, *halushechky pshen-ychnye* are wheaten dumplings, *pampushechy* are buns, and *tovchenychky* are fish or meat buns (or dumplings)." See Natalia M. Kolb-Seletski, "Gastronomy, Gogol, and His Fiction," *Slavic Review*, March 1970, p. 53.

4. In Chapter 2 of "The Terrible Boar," Katherine supposes that Onisko has come to see her father. Onisko remarks that he would be a fool to take "lenten kasha" with "dumplings [*vareniki*] in sour cream" before his "very nose" (III:271). She seems uncertain "how to understand his words," and Onisko explains that he would be misguided to seek "the father, when there is such a very pretty daughter."

5. This and several episodes discussed below are treated somewhat differently in my "Observations Relating to Black Humor in Gogol and Nabokov," *Slavic and East European Journal*, Vol. 18, No. 4.

6. A peddler woman strangely suspects this, though she has no idea of the red jacket's "true" history. She even calls it "demon's clothing" (when it will not burn), and a peasant (its next possessor) decides it was foisted upon him by "evil hands" (127).

7. Three bits of the red jacket are apparently planted to fool Solopy and Havronya.

"ST. JOHN'S EVE"

At first glance, this seems to be a moralistic horror story about the tragic results of pursuing worldly riches. In order to marry the lovely Pidorka, whose father Korzh wishes her to wed a rich Pole, Petrus makes a bargain with the evil Basavryuk. The deal brings him both gold and Pidorka, but it also leads him to kill her little brother Ivas, his faithful friend. In the end, Petrus and his riches are destroyed by evil forces, and Pidorka is said to be living in a convent. Basavryuk, now apparently revealed as Satan himself, continues to terrify the village.

The story may be seen as a series of deceptive appearances, with Gogol focusing upon the treacherous surface of reality. We are told in the introduction that the sacristan is "deathly averse" to retelling a tale the same way. If persuaded to retell, he alters the story "so that it cannot be recognized" (I:137). As Vsevolod Setchkarev has observed, this presumably alludes to the drastic editing inflicted upon "St. John's Eve" when Gogol first published it.[1] But it is also true that late in the story, both Petrus and Pidorka are separately said to have altered until they cannot be recognized (148,149). When Basavryuk first appears, he is calmly termed "a person, or better, a devil in human form" (139). ("Better" is Gogol's favorite reversal word.[2]) And at the climax, Petrus obeys a witch and kills Ivas upon seeing a fortune of gold and jewels beneath the surface of the earth, which has suddenly become as transparent as crystal.

"St. John's Eve" contains numerous hints that a sinister substructure influences the surface of reality. The sacristan's first sentence contains a matter-of-fact reference to "the other world." And he soon presumes that "emigrants from the other world" are apt to place themselves "on your bed." Then, as the action begins, we read:

> once—well, it's already clear that no one else but the evil one got hold of him—it occurred to Petrus, without looking about carefully in the front hall, to smack a kiss, as they say, from all his soul upon the little pink lips of the cossack girl, and the very same evil one—may he dream, son of a dog, of the holy cross —inveigled the old geezer out of stupidity to open the door of

his hut. Korzh turned to wood, his mouth gaping and his hand clutching the door. The accursed kiss, it seemed, had stupified him completely.

This passage contains several Gogolian themes (a father's intense closeness to his daughter; an interrupted intimacy; [3] a frozen pose with mouth agape; and the devil's sly influence in everyday life). The point of view is also Gogolian: a slightly alien observer seems to be relating this scene. To whom is it "already clear" that the devil incited Petrus? To whom did it "seem" that the accursed kiss stupified Korzh? The passage is faintly echoed, moreover, by the last sentence of the story, wherein the devil, once again parenthetically termed "the son of a dog," causes flocks of birds to rise screeching into the sky.

Gogolian interlocking details subtly reinforce the plot. Early in the story, we read that "poor Petrus owned nothing more than one gray jacket, which had more holes in it than a Jew has gold coins in his pocket." (141). Though the holes may well be round, like coins, the comparison is still somewhat unsettling. For it (reversely) employs an image of wealth to describe extreme poverty. Yet there are other factors. As a stereotyped miser, the Jew may live quite poorly in order to increase his wealth, which with precarious logic renders the comparison strangely appropriate. And as the holes are likened to coins in a pocket, the owner seems faintly vulnerable to losing them. As the plot develops, we see that Petrus's devil's money does not prevent disaster; in fact, the money is finally lost.

When Petrus obtains the money, he is seized by a deathly sleep for two days and two nights. Awakening, he can remember nothing: "his memory was like the pocket of an old miser, out of which you cannot wheedle a penny" (146). Once again, we have the image of a pocket bulging with seemingly inaccessible coins. At this point, Petrus discovers his two sacks of devil's gold. His sudden wealth thus seems faintly undermined by a double image of apparently useless riches.

Other details strangely interact. Petrus, we learn, was called "the Kinless," possible because no one remembered his parents (140). Someone tried to trace his relatives, "but Petrus had as much need of them as he did of last year's snow." The comparison seems oddly appropriate: both parents and snow have melted away without a trace. "Last year's snow," moreover, has connotations of seasons and cycles. The two most terrible scenes in the story (the killings of Ivas and of Petrus) both occur on St. John's Eves. The story also seems rounded by the fact that Bisavryuk is the first main character to be presented, and he is indirectly featured (as the devil) in the closing sentence as he scares the flocks of birds.

Petrus grows desperate for riches when Korzh seems about to force Pidorka to marry "a certain Pole, trimmed in gold, with a moustache, a sword, spurs, and pockets jangling like the sound of the sack with which our sexton Taras sets out every day for the church" (142). Here, a third image of a pocket bulging with coins soon comes to naught, for despite the Pole's courtship, Petrus wins Pidorka. (The jangling sack of coins is echoed later, when Basavryuk, in order to entice Petrus into their agreement, jangles his purse.)

The Pole disappears. After Petrus murders Ivas, he suffers a prolonged depression and loss of memory. Then winter comes: "Here already on a clear, frosty day the red-breasted bullfinch, like a rather dandified Polish nobleman, was strutting about in the heaps of snow, pulling out seed . . ." (149). This playful return of the rich Pole is subtly ironic, for he searches in snow, which has already been established as suggesting a futile search for kin. The word "bullfinch" *(snegir')* contains a play on "snow" *(sneg)*. Even the bird's quest for "seed" may be seen in ironic connection with the Pole's futile courtship of Pidorka. And it also seems faintly pertinent that the story ends with a picture of wildly frightened birds, chased away by the devil as was the Pole by the appearance of the devil's gold.

While "St. John's Eve" seems to be a moralistic horror story, it also seems strangely fatalistic. Although Petrus makes at least two apparently free choices, agreeing to the deal with Basavryuk and then disregarding the latter's admonition not to pick "even one" flower, he appears to be quite helpless: Korzh seeks a rich husband for Pidorka. One almost suspects that a hidden history (as in "The Terrible Vengeance") finally explains the plight of Petrus—that he is doomed, perhaps, for a crime committed by one of his ancestors and destined to be known as "The Kinless."

Pidorka seems tinged with unearthly evil. She is first described as a typical Gogolian beauty, glowing and faintly transparent: "the young cossack girl's plumpish cheeks were clear and fresh, like a poppy of the most delicate pink color, when, bathed with God's dew, it burns, straightening up its petals and preening itself before the warm, new-risen sun. . . " (141). When Petrus decides to pick the forbidden flower, it is described as follows: "All of a sudden, a little flower bud started to turn red and , as if alive, moved. . . . It moved and kept growing bigger, turning red as a hot coal. . . . the flower opened before his eyes like a flame. . . " (144). The double image of a burning flower serves to reinforce the fact that Petrus will now obtain the devil's gold in order to marry Pidorka. In Russian, where the word "alive" is feminine (because "bud" is feminine), the identification of girl and flower seems still more likely. The "burning" of course tends to tinge both flower and Pidorka with evil. And soon we read that Petrus's eyes "began to burn" at the sight of the treasure, whereupon he kills Ivas, after which "the trees, all in blood, it seemed, were burning" (146). Finally, all this seems reflected in an apparently unrelated Gogolian detail: the sacristan recalls an especially "merry" [4] wedding at which someone, prompted by the devil, poured vodka over one of the women and set her afire (148).

Notes

1. Vsevolod Setchkarev, *Gogol: His Life and Works* (New York, 1965), p. 99.

2. See my "Gogolesque Perception-Expanding Reversals in Nabokov," pp. 111-12. In a reworked scene from *Vladimir, Third Class* entitled "Fragment," one character declares: "my son fell in love, or, better [*luchshe*], didn't fall in love but simply got crazy in the head . . . " (V:131).

3. In Chapter Two of "The Terrible Boar," Onisko is showering Katherine (during her father's absence) with kisses, when "a clear, piercing voice more terrible than thunder" rings out (III:275). It is Simoniha, who has been watching—a typical unseen audience.

4. In another typical reversal, the sacristan expresses astonishment at a widespread "unbelief": he had recently met a person who "does not trust witches" (139). Later, of course, a witch induces Petrus to murder Ivas.

"MAY NIGHT, OR THE DROWNED MAIDEN"

It is dusk in the village. Young people are singing gay sounds which, the narration presumes, always suggest despondency. "And the pensive evening was dreamily embracing the blue sky, transforming everything into vagueness and distance." (I:153). So begins the story, with a reversal of emotion and a transformation resulting from an embrace.

Levko, a young cossack and son of the village Head, plays a bandora outside a peasant cottage. Finally a girl named Ganna comes out. "In the half-clear murkiness, her bright eyes were burning with welcome like little stars. . . ." Levko repeatedly embraces and kisses her. Ganna exclaims that the water is "swaying" very "quietly." She is looking at a pond: "Like a feeble old man, it held the distant dark sky in its cold embrace, showering with icy kisses the fiery stars . . ." (156).[1] Blending in with the lovers' "flowery, peculiar, and exotic style of speaking,"[2] these words anticipate much of the story. For the pond is later revealed to hold in its cold embrace a multitude of drowned maidens. (This is of course another transformation following an embrace; in retrospect, Levko's repeated embracing of Ganna may perhaps faintly suggest that she, too, is not exactly what she seems.) Also in conjunction with the pond description, the famous opening of Part Two ("Do you know the Ukrainian night? O, you do not know the Ukrainian night!") later acquires a deeper meaning as the drowned maidens issue from the pond for the ghostly nocturnal scene. Even the title of the story, often unfortunately shortened in English, slyly suggests this superimposing of realities: "May Night, or The Drowned Maiden." Also traceable to the initial pond description, an old widower takes a young wife in the background story explaining the ghostly pond scene. And Ganna, whose eyes were described as "burning" like "stars," is later revealed to be intimate with Levko's father, who thus seems suggested by the "old man" kissing "fiery stars" in the pond which fascinates Ganna.

There are various hints that Ganna loves Levko's father. For example, she becomes intensely interested in the father's reaction when Levko told him of their love. Also, Levko tells Ganna a story

that features female treachery. "Trust women!" he tells her sarcas-
tically (158).[3] And when Ganna first appears to Levko, we read that
"from the lad's eagle eyes not even the blush, modestly flaring up on
her cheeks, could conceal itself." While it is hardly apparent in
context, the girl presumably blushes not only from appearing to her
lover, but also because she is intimate with his father as well. Thus,
what "cannot hide" is also that which does. The word "modestly,"
moreover, tends to reverse its meaning, and "even" stresses Levko's
perceptiveness while being deceived.

Levko's father is the Village Head, which Gogol amusingly exploits. (The Head turns up his nose, the Head tramples people with
his feet, and so on.) When Levko surprises Ganna with another man
at night, he strains to discover the identity of his rival: "a shadow
covered him from feet to head" (162). Levko has no idea that it is the
Head. (The Head is repeatedly termed "the stranger." [4])

Other examples of Gogolian false focus may be found in the
description of the Head's sister-in-law.

> The Head was a widower, but in his house lived his sister-in-
> law . . . In the village, they said she was not his relative at all;
> but we have already seen . . . much slander. However, . . . the
> sister-in-law was always displeased if the Head dropped in on
> a cossack who had a young daughter. . . . He would not train
> his eye on a fetching little face, however, before looking about
> carefully to see whether his sister-in-law was watching from
> somewhere. (161)

The woman is repeatedly called "sister-in-law" just as we become
increasingly certain that she is not. (Or, more precisely, we realize
amid these repetitions that the sister-in-law's role is not that of a
sister-in-law, even if she really is a sister-in-law.) And if the "cossack" is visited because of his "young daughter," we may also note
here a tinge of false focus.

Later, as the young people of the village disguise themselves and
run wild, abusing the Head, the sister-in-law is twice mistaken for
one of the revelers. When first captured, the prisoner "peacefully"
follows the Head "as if into his own house" (169). Despite this hint,
few readers will realize the prisoner's identity at this point. "His

own" *(svoyu)* is especially ironic, since the sister-in-law seems to be living as the Head's wife. In the second episode, she is slyly substituted for a prisoner, and the Head nearly has her burnt as a witch. Together, these two instances form a double image of confused identity quite appropriate to the sister-in-law's ambiguous role.

The story that Levko tells Ganna explains how a girl, hated by her stepmother-witch, drowned herself. As a water nymph, she then pulled her stepmother into the pond, but the witch disguised herself as one of the numerous drowned maidens. Earlier, when the witch turns her husband against her daughter, he orders the girl to do numerous chores and to keep away from his bedroom: "It was hard for the poor girl, but nothing could be done: she set to fulfilling her father's will" (157). This "will," of course, is really the witch's. The false focus seems especially ironic because the father had claimed that after his marriage he would caress his daughter even more than before.

The first night after her arrival, the witch retires with her husband and then appears in the form of a "terrible black cat" to frighten her stepdaughter. (Hence, we have still another transformation following an embrace.) The cat stalks the girl "with iron claws" and tries to strangle her, but she cuts off one paw with her father's sword. The next day, the stepmother appears with a bandaged hand, which seems to suggest an overlapping of two realities (in much the same way that a note to the Head does later). And the cat's "iron claws" anticipate Levko's visionlike dream: he detects the disguised witch when she seems to grow claws in the "ravens" game (176).

The witch's "cat" role seems echoed by two apparently unrelated descriptions. First, there is the distiller's moustache: "Short, thick whiskers stuck out beneath his nose; but flashing only vaguely through the tobacco smoke, they seemed like a mouse which the distiller had caught and was holding in his mouth, disrupting the monopoly of the granary cat" (165). Later, the Head stealthily tries to capture some youths who are singing disrespectful songs outside his window: "Thus only an old experienced cat sometimes allows an inexperienced mouse to run around his tail, while actually he is quickly forming a plan about how to cut off its way back to its hole" (168). In both these descriptions, a cat temporarily fails to capture its prey (the daughter cut off the witch's paw), but the prey is nevertheless doomed (the daughter drowns).

Ending his story, Levko embraces Ganna, kisses her, and leaves. "Good-bye, Levko!" she says. Almost immediately, several youths slip up next to her in the dark. "Good-bye, Ganna!" they say, pretending to be Levko, embracing and furtively kissing her "from all sides." One of them later attempts to repeat the joke, but his lips encounter the Head's rough whiskers in the darkness; thus, we have still another transformation following an embrace.

All this furtive evening kissing is reinforced by a double image which takes shape in the background narration. In the famous "Ukrainian night" description, we read of the "virginal groves" of cherry trees: "the night wind, having stolen up momentarily, kisses them" (159). Later, the drowned maidens at the pond are quite casually likened to "a riverside reed, touched at the quiet hour of twilight by the airy lips of the wind" (176).

Other interlocking details in "May Night, or The Drowned Maiden" serve to unite the two halves of the title. The Ukrainian night description focuses first upon the moon, then upon the moon's "silvery light," and then we read: "Heavenly night!" (159). Both the village and the people are said to be asleep, and the drunken Kalenik is pictured trying to find his way home.

All these details are explicitly contained in the final nine lines of the story: the Ukrainian night sky, the moon, its silvery shining, the words "heavenly night," the sleeping village, and the drunken Kalenik, searching for his cottage (180). Together, these descriptions form a double image that surrounds and intensifies the "drowned maiden" scene in Levko's dream. "He looked about him: the night seemed even more brilliant. Some kind of strange, intoxicating radiance was added to the shining of the moon. Never before had he chanced to see anything like it. A silvery mist was falling all around" (174). Framed by two similar scenes of intoxicating nocturnal brilliance, this "unreal" one seems almost to exist, unnoticed, in the "real" world. And when the drowned maidens appear, this background tends to render their reality both timeless and strangely familiar.

This seems especially so because Gogol deftly interweaves the two realities in Levko's dream. At one point, he gazes at the shore of the pond: "in the fine silvery mist there flitted light, as if shadows, maidens in white, like a meadow dotted with lilies-of-the-valley, chemises; . . . they were pale; their bodies looked molded from transparent clouds and seemed illuminated through by the silvery moonlight" (176). Comparisons from the "real" world (shadows, meadow, flowers) seem to show through this description of the supernatural. The word order has been quite strictly maintained to illustrate that its "broken" arrangement contributes to the uncanny, patchy effect. Glimpses of the real seem visible within the supernatural, and the silvery moonlight seems to exist simultaneously in two separate but overlapping realities.[5]

Tricked by some village girls, the drunken Kalenik is about to enter the Head's house, thinking it his own: "Before Kalenik reaches the end of his journey, we will, without doubt, succeed in saying something about him" (160). The immediate joke is that narration continues for almost six pages before Kalenik opens the door. But since he barges into the Head's house, the drunk has by no means "reached the end of his journey." Indeed he is still searching for it as the story ends.[6]

"May Night" contains numerous ironic reversals. The distiller, for instance, terms the drunken Kalenik a "useful" person. The distiller suggests punishing a reveler by forcing him to work in the distillery, or, "better," by hanging him. And after his fantastic visionlike dream, Levko decides to conceal the "real" truth of how he got the note. (The humorous lie he concocts seems more credible than this "real" truth.)

One such reversal is both sly and complex. When Kalenik first appears, drunkenly dancing along in quest of his cottage, some peasant girls offer to help him but insist that he must "dance on ahead" (160). Kalenik answers by calling them "scheming girls." On one level, they may be seen as "scheming" in order to counter the schemes they attribute to Kalenik. Yet they proceed to trick Kalenik into entering not his own, but the Head's house, after which he drunkenly abuses the Head, who hears everything he says. Kalenik's reversed epithet thus proves ironically true, reinforcing the effect of Levko's sarcastic pronouncement: "Trust women!"

Notes

1. Since the word "pond" is masculine in Russian, "it" and "its" are actually "he" and "his."

2. See Setcharev, p. 102.

3. The word *verit'* ("to trust, to believe") is similarly employed in "St. John's Eve" (for witches) and in "Nevsky Prospect" (for beautiful women and the street itself).

4. Here, a Gogolian purposeful redundancy suggests the slow, vague process of Levko's near recognition: "it seemed to the lad that the voice of the stranger was not entirely unfamiliar, and it was as if he had heard it somewhere."

5. In "The Lost Letter," "Gogol uses his technique of broken description when a devil magically provides a steed for the grandfather: "A devil cracked a whip—a horse, like fire, rose up beneath him, and grandfather, birdlike, was borne upward." (190) In this case, the choppy wording suggests both the abruptness of the devil's magic and its effect upon the startled grandfather.

6. In *Dead Souls,* Gogol creates a similar ironic twist when Chichikov visits Manilov: "Although the time in the course of which they will be crossing the threshold, front hall, and dining room is rather short, we shall nevertheless try to make use of it to say something about the master of the house" (VI:23). Here, the immediate joke is that they seem to spend almost four pages completing these enumerated actions. Actually, they have been standing at the living room door "for several minutes" when we return to them, so the time it took them to get there really was "rather short."

"THE LOST LETTER"

The hero of this story is the sacristan's grandfather, who has dealings with the devil which seem to leave an evil influence upon his house. By inference, then, the sacristan's holiness also seems faintly tainted at the end. As Setchkarev has observed, the hero "is constantly designated as grandfather, while his actions are not at all grandfatherly—this contrast produces the desired comic effect." [1] A smiliar Gogolian false focus centers on the grandfather's cap. Since the letter (to the Tsaritsa herself) is hidden in this cap, references to the cap are of course more significantly to the letter.

The Gogolian title expands in meaning as the story progresses. The word "lost" (*propavshaya*) also means "vanished." Upon receiving the letter, grandfather hurriedly sews it into his cap, where it stays until the very end of the tale. The letter is thus not visible ("vanished") for a considerable time both before and after it is "lost" (stolen.)

The Gogolian plot of the story is simple to outline, exceedingly complex as developed in narrative detail. Having sewn the letter in his cap, grandfather stops at a fair, where he drinks deep with a cossack, falls asleep, and loses his cap. At the advice of a tavern keeper, he meets some devils and witches in a nearby forest and gambles for his cap, which he wins only by making the sign of the cross over the cards. He awakens at home, where his wife is seated on a bench, strangely bouncing and seeing a weird dream. He delivers the letter and is rewarded, but at the same time each year, his wife's legs begin compulsively dancing.

In the sacristan's rambling introduction, we are told that people bowed to grandfather because he was literate, and in those days all the literate folk in Baturin would not even fill up your cap (I:182). We then learn that grandfather, selected as messenger to the Tsaritsa, hides the letter inside his cap. The hypothetical cap (containing literate folk) is thus an appropriate anticipation of the real one (containing the letter). In Russian, the words used for "literate folk" and "letter" seem even closer (*gramoteev, gramota*).

As they drink together at the fair, the cossack (presumably a disguised devil [2]) exchanges caps with grandfather. The cossack then claims he has made a deal with the devil and asks grandfather to guard him at night. Grandfather declares he would rather have the long forelock cut from his own head than let the devil do in his new friend (184). This image of lost forelock ironically prefigures the loss of his cap, which vanishes, along with the cossack, when grandfather falls asleep. He awakens and discovers his loss only "when the sun had already thoroughly baked the shaved crown of his head" (184). With Gogolian precarious logic, the sun seems almost to burn into his (capless) head the intelligence that the cap is lost. And no matter how much grandfather scratched the back of his head," he could think of no way out of the situation. Thus the loss of his cap, prefigured by his own unwitting "forelock" reference, is supplemented by a double image of appropriate "head" descriptions. At the end of the story, moreover, the Tsaritsa orders that a cap be filled with money as a reward for grandfather.

Also in his introduction, the sacristan claims to be plagued by village girls and young women who love his tales. "Of course I don't mind telling them stories," he says, "but you just look at what happens to them in bed. Why, I know that each one trembles under a blanket as if seized by a fever, and would be glad to crawl under her sheepskin coat, head and all." Leaving the fair, grandfather and his cossack drinking companion ride out into the country at sunset: "before them spread colorful cornfields, like the holiday petticoats of dark-browed young women." After the sunset, the entire sky closes over "with night, as with black cloth," and in the fields it becomes "exactly as dark as under a sheepskin coat."

When grandfather enters the forest, as advised by the tavern keeper: "It was dark and muffled, as in a wine cellar; one could only hear, far, far above, over one's head, a cold wind carousing in the treetops, and the trees, like drunken cossack heads, were loosely shaking, whispering with their leaves a tipsy refrain" (186). At this point, it suddenly turns so cold that "grandfather thought of his sheepskin coat." This seemingly casual detail may recall the girls who trembled feverishly and would have been glad to crawl under a sheepskin coat. Soon after this, we read that any Christian would have started "trembling" at the mere sight of how the witches and devils danced: "like drunken people." Gogol thus establishes a series of images involving trembling, drunken shaking, dancing and nocturnal fright. And all this seems in strange harmony with the ending: when grandfather returns home, his children are crying: "Look, look, mother's jumping like crazy!" He finds her sitting and bouncing on a bench," asleep. And as the story ends, we learn that she mysteriously has to dance at the same time every year, as if her legs were abruptly jerked, by evil forces, against her will.

This, the narrator presumes, was a punishment because grandfather forgot to have his hut blessed after his wife's eerie experience. She had dreamed "that a stove was traveling about the hut, chasing out with a spade the pots, tubs, and the devil knows what else" (190-91). Gogol typically inserts a casual phrase about the devil at a rather suggestive moment. As the grandfather tells his wife: "You got it in a dream; I, while awake." But why, we may wonder, was it the stove that came alive?

As mentioned above, the grandfather's cossack "friend" seems to be a disguised devil who exchanges caps to steal the letter. While they celebrate, the cossack talks so wildly that "a demon" seems to be "inside him" (183). When at last he quiets down, it is said that he looks like he wants to go home and lie on the stove. The devil's home is of course hell; and as "Red" Panko explains in his Preface, the word *peklo* (with the same root as *pech'*, "stove") means "hell." *Peklo* appears twice in "The Lost Letter," once in conjunction with the devil and once with the witches and devils in the forest, when grandfather thinks he may almost be "in hell itself" (185,187). Thus, when his wife sees "the stove" chasing "the devil knows what" out of their hut, her dream seems to complete a series of hidden allusions.[3] If so, the grandfather's conclusion ("You got it in a dream; I, while awake") takes on an eerie hue of literal truth.

Finally, "The Lost Letter" contains numerous reversals. The tavern keeper declares that money is a "goodness" of which both people and the devil are fond (186). The terrifying forest scene is described as "not altogether cheery" (186). With the devils and witches, grandfather eats ham with a fork "hardly any smaller" than the forks with which peasants pitch hay (188). Similarly, he decides that one of the witches is their leader because she seems "just a bit prettier than all the rest" (188). Most typical of all is the notion of "treating" someone to angry abuse (185).[4]

Notes

1. Setchkarev, pp. 104-05.
2. See Setchkarev, p. 105.
3. In addition, the witches ride on "pokers"; grandfather asks the devils for a light, whereupon they push a "firebrand" in his face; and he is being "baked" *(pripeklo)* by the sun when he awakens to his loss (185,187,184).
4. See also I:114,164,213,313.

"PREFACE TO PART TWO"

"Here is another little book for you," Panko begins, "or better to say, the last one." The reversal word "better" humorously undermines the very product presented. Yet it also seems rather appropriate: Panko, we learn, has already been ridiculed locally.

Predominantly gray-haired "Red" Panko then admonishes the reader not "to cuss out" him or his book: "It is not nice to cuss while parting, especially with someone, God only knows if you will meet soon again." Panko thus achieves the reversallike feat of bidding the reader farewell at the beginning of his Preface.

Most of the Preface then features a person who "has been gone for a long time." This is the man in the pea-green jacket, who (in the Preface to Part One) had supposedly exhibited self-control by remaining silent for some time when displeased (I:106). Here we are told of an incident that took place before the man departed. During a syllogistically presented conversation about how to salt apples,[1] Panko had remarked that the man's notion of sprinkling grass over the apples could elicit ridicule. "What would you think he answered to that? Nothing! spat on the floor, took his cap and left." Remembering the man's former behavior, one could well expect this supposedly surprising silence. The man's conduct, moreover, exactly fulfills Panko's earlier admonishment to the reader: "It is not nice to cuss while parting, especially with someone, God only knows if you will meet soon again." This man, we recall, "has been gone for a long time." All this attention to the man after he has gone may be seen as a rather typical false focus.

Panko emphatically decides the man's departure was "so much the better," for "there is nothing worse in the world than these high-class people." The man's uncle, it seems, was a snobbish commisar. "As if commisar is such a high rank, that there are none higher in the world? Thank God, there are higher ranks than commisar. No, I do not like these high-class people." Panko thus (reversely) demonstrates his dislike for high-class people by thanking God for even higher ones. His words suggest that "it serves them right" to be outranked, an idea that points up his own ill-concealed respect for the power of high-ranking people.

Finally, Panko apologizes for not including, as he had promised before, his own story: three such books would now be needed. Actually, the "promise" in his first Preface was qualified by "perhaps" (106), with the further suggestion that his "damned laziness" might interfere. At that time, he claimed to have enough material for ten such books. Here, Panko exclaims: "Good-bye! We shall not see each other for a long time, perhaps not at all." The "Preface" thus contains yet another farewell.

Notes

1. The conversation, we are led to believe, is: (1) not about trifles; (2) about salting apples; (3) interrupted.

"CHRISTMAS EVE"

The devil lusts for revenge upon the blacksmith Vacula, who once painted a religious mural demeaning the Evil Spirit. Vacula plans to visit the beautiful Oksana while her father, the rich cossack Chub, is away at a Christmas Eve celebration. To prevent Chub's leaving, the devil creates a dissuasive darkness by stealing the moon unobserved. "True, the district clerk, coming out of a tavern on all fours, saw the moon dancing in the sky for no reason whatsoever . . . but the villagers shook their heads and even made fun of him" (I:203). This typical reversal of sober and intoxicated vision [1] effectively reinforces the play of meaning in "true."

Having slipped the moon into his pocket, the devil meets Vacula's mother Soloha, who is also a witch, riding in the sky. "The witch, seeing herself suddenly in darkness, shrieked" (204). Gogol's use of "seeing" has an eerie tinge, suggesting perhaps that witches can indeed see in the dark.

Like a human lover, the devil puts his arm around the witch, whispering into Soloha's ear "the very same that is usually whispered to the entire female sex." At this point, we encounter the exclamation: "Things are strangely arranged in our world!" As developed, this introduces a Gogolian digression about how people try to copy and surpass each other in wearing fine clothes. And even the devil, we read, emulates the amorous ways of people, which is especially "vexing" because this ugly creature "surely" imagines himself to be handsome. This faintly eerie point of view ("surely" [2]) presumes a human insight into the devil's thoughts and feelings which balances the devil's quite human behavior. As Setchkarev puts it, the realistic and the fantastic are blended here as a matter of course.[3] And the phrase "strangely arranged in our world" contains a typical false focus: "our" world expands with a sinister suggestiveness.

Especially in this story, Gogol's blending of at least two realities is abetted by an abrupt shifting back and forth from one scene to another. In result, one scene tends to linger in the reader's mind while another is described. Here, the picture of ugly devil playing gallant lover suddenly fades away: "it became so dark that abso-

lutely nothing could be seen that took place further between them."
This comic, interrupted love scene anticipates several others, also
narrated with a faintly eerie point of view.

Focus abruptly shifts to Chub, who is setting out for the Christmas Eve celebration when the moon vanishes. "What the devil!" he
exclaims. Having no idea of the devil's plan to keep him home, he
then abuses the devil for "meddling."

Still, Chub continues on his way, while we observe Oksana at
home. Admiring herself in the mirror, this spoiled beauty declares:
"People lie, I'm not pretty at all."

> But the fresh, childishly animated face that flashed in the
> mirror with its dark shining eyes and inexpressably pleasant
> smirk, which burned through one's soul, suddenly proved the
> opposite. (207)

Even as Oksana's playfully denied beauty is confirmed, Gogol adds
the word "opposite" (*protivnoe*), which can also mean "repulsive."
This submeaning enlarges as Oksana likens her curls to "long
snakes" winding around her head. After this, she revels in the
"miracle" of her beauty, supposing that the man she marries will
kiss her "to death." Here, as in "The Sorochintsy Fair," we abruptly
discover that the beauty who watches herself in the mirror was also
being watched by someone else. Vacula has already arrived. The
observation, when Oksana was apparently alone, about her eyes
"burning through one's soul" may thus be seen as Vacula's reaction.
Later, he thinks to himself that her gaze "burns and burns" (221).
Vacula now decides to kiss Oksana "a million times" (208), but she
denies him. "Give you some honey, and you need a spoon too," she
says, pushing him away. They are soon interrupted by a knock at the
door.

Focus shifts to the devil, who has hotly followed "his mistress"
down the chimney into her cottage. The witch quickly peeks out of
the stove to see if her son Vacula has guests. Observing "that there
was no one, excepting only the sacks which were lying near the
middle of the hut," she emerges as Soloha.

Here we receive a brief description of Soloha. It begins with
Gogol's "neither-nor" device (later used repeatedly to depict Chi-

chikov): "She was neither good-looking nor ugly." But Soloha, we read, was habitually visited by several male villagers who had "little need for beauty."

> And to her honor it can be said that she could dispense with them artfully. Not to any one of them did it occur that he had a rival. (211)

This passage promotes a most unusual definition of "honor." [4] Humor also derives from the understatement "a rival," which could be called a quantitative false focus. And Soloha's "artfulness" in dispensing with her lovers is soon amply demonstrated: when they visit her, she hides each successive caller in the coal sacks lying on the floor. This develops further the theme of interrupted intimacy with an eerie point of view: as the sacks fill up, an unseen (and unseeing) audience slowly accumulates to hear the next visitor's advances. The sacks grow almost literally human. Soloha had observed, we may recall, that there was "no one" in the hut "excepting only the sacks." Similarly, the casual words "his mistress" (when the devil followed Soloha home) humorously expand in meaning as we learn that she is also the mistress of many others.[5] Gogol adds still another touch of prophetic irony when Soloha first sees the sacks and decides to leave them where they are. "Vacula brought them in; let him take them out himself!" she resolves. Later, he does exactly this, unaware that the sacks now contain "human" coal.

Before Soloha's visitors arrive, focus shifts to Chub, stubbornly en route with no moon to light his way. The devil has briefly returned to stir up a snowstorm. "Ugh, what a heap of snow Satan has thrown in my eyes!" exclaims Chub with customary ironic accuracy. Blinded by the blizzard, Chub returns to his own cottage, interrupting his daughter and Vacula. Hearing the blacksmith's voice, he presumes that Vacula is visiting the young wife of another man, the only other villager with a house that resembles his own. Pummeled by Vacula, Chub heads back into the snowstorm.

As the devil returns to Soloha, the moon slips out of his pocket to its rightful place in the sky. Oksana and the blacksmith join the young people to sing Christmas carols. Before these witnesses, Oksana playfully promises to marry Vacula if he brings her the Tsaritsa's slippers. Leaving amid a chorus of laughter, Vacula decides not to try: Oksana does not love him, nor is she the only girl in the village. But just as the blacksmith decides "to be resolute" (216), he again pictures Oksana and changes his mind. The reversal word "resolute" (which refers to his resolve to abandon his resolve) increases in irony as Vacula returns to his initial resolution.

The devil has meanwhile been making advances to Soloha in earnest. She is termed "not so cruel" as to deny him; besides, they were alone. Soloha, we read, "was rarely without company; this evening, however, she was planning to spend alone" because her male friends would be at the Christmas Eve party. "Alone" now seems to mean "with the amorous devil." Because of successive interruptions, however, Soloha really does remain "alone," as far as love making is concerned. At this point, the "company" she "was rarely without" begins to arrive.

Interrupted by the village Head, the devil hastily hides in one of the coal sacks. Also interrupted by a knock at the door, the Head crawls into another sack. In this way, both the devil and Head constitute a live background for the clerk's advances:

He walked up to her closer, coughed, grinned, and with his long fingers touched her full, bare arm and pronounced, with a look expressing both slyness and self-satisfaction:

"And what is this you have, glorious Soloha?" Then, having spoken, he jumped back a little.

"What is it? Why, an arm, Osip Nikiforovich," answered Soloha.

"Hmm, an arm, heh, heh," said the clerk, heartily content with his beginning, and took a little walk around the room.

"And what do you have here, dearest Soloha?" he pronounced with the very same look, having approached her once more, grasped her neck lightly with his hand, and jumped back in the very same manner.

"As if you didn't see, Osip Nikiforovich!" answered Soloha. "A neck, with a coin necklace on it."

"Hmm, with a coin necklace on it, heh, heh," and the clerk took another little walk around the room, rubbing his hands.

"And what do you have here, incomparable Soloha?" It is

not known what the clerk would have touched with his long
fingers now, since a knock was suddenly heard at the door. . . .
(217-18)

The clerk makes three advances—to Soloha's arm, to her neck, and
somewhere else. The first two times, he touches and then questions.
In the second approach, however, word order is reversed: we encounter his question before learning that he had already touched
(and even jumped back). Then, the third time, even the actual
chronology is reversed: the clerk first questions and, interrupted,
never touches. But the focus is clearly upon his "rubbing hands" and
the repeated phrase "with his long fingers." Accustomed to the
pattern of touching and then questioning, we therefore tend to
picture him as having touched . . . what? Just before, negation
ironically aided us in picturing Soloha's neck ("As if you didn't see,
Osip Nikiforovich!"). Now, the words "incomparable" and "it is not
known" ironically vivify the last (unrealized) touch: its location
seems either "very much known" or at least amusingly unimportant.
Especially because reversed chronology places the question first
("And what do you have here . . . ?"), we tend to picture the last
touch as having occurred.

Generally, the passage evokes a faintly alien uneasiness. It con-
trasts the clerk's personal desire (*his* long fingers . . . *self*-satisfaction
. . . *his* beginning . . . *his* long fingers) with Soloha's strangely im-
personal desirableness (an arm . . . a neck . . . it is not known).
Moreover, the clerk's brazen advances seem almost like squeamish
retreats. Still another reversal is contained in the verb used for the
second amorous advance *(pristupiv)*, which has a submeaning of
"setting about a task." And of course the uneasy atmosphere is
intensified because both the devil and the Head are muffled witnesses of the couple's unusual intimacies.

Victor Shklovsky has suggested that this passage exemplifies the
descriptive technique of "defamiliarization" or "making strange." [6]
While it is true that Gogol's technique here ironically vivifies certain
parts of Soloha's body, the method nevertheless differs in two ways
from "normal" defamiliarization. First, the reader's perception is
impeded more by interrupted action than by unfamiliar designation
(referring, say, to Soloha's "apples" instead of her "breasts"). The

second Gogolian twist involves the characters' perceptions. Both
Soloha and the clerk, one infers, are familiar indeed with what is
occurring. The clerk's experience, as related, could perhaps be
termed "mock defamiliarization." However, due to the various factors (described above) which promote an atmosphere of faintly alien
uneasiness, one senses that the narrative consciousness itself has
replaced a character's in being unfamiliar with what it perceives. In
short, the narration need not "make strange" if a situation already
seems so.

When they are interrupted, "virtuous" Soloha hides the clerk in
another coal sack. His "not too massive body" settles on the very
bottom, "so that on top of it one could have poured still another
half-sack of coal." This casual statement slyly anticipates the fact
that Chub will hide in the same sack, on top of the clerk. The false
focus (of still more "coal") is especially appropriate because Vacula
will carry out the "human coal," also as prefigured. Here, Chub
enters.

Before an unseen audience of three, Chub inquires: Perhaps Soloha did not expect him? Perhaps he has interrupted something?
Perhaps she was having fun with someone? Perhaps he is hidden?
All this, Chub utters "inwardly triumphing that only he enjoyed
Soloha's favors." He then proposes a drink of vodka, exclaiming
what a night God has sent on Christmas Eve. (The reversal word
"God" seems obvious, but for full effect we must remember that the
devil, who has been tampering with the night, is hidden just a few
feet away.)

A voice cries "Open!" and Chub, in a panic, becomes the additional "half-sack of coal" above the clerk. Vacula enters. At this
point, Soloha has still another visitor, whom she leads out into the
back yard. Left "alone," Vacula wonders: "What are these sacks
lying here for? It was time to take them away long ago. Through this
stupid love I've become a dunce. Tomorrow's a holiday, and in the
hut lies all kinds of trash" (219). Now the ironies pour from Vacula's
lips. Especially versatile are his words that he has become "a dunce
through stupid love." "What the devil," he exclaims, "these sacks
seem heavier than before!" (Again, the devil must be pictured
for full effect.) And although Vacula suspects that someone has
"surely" added something besides coal, he reconsiders and calls

himself an idiot: loads now seem heavier than when he was younger.

Carrying the sack that contains the devil, Vacula leaves his hut, determined not to take a wife. He soon encounters Oksana, who displays "that same smirk which almost drove him mad." As before, he seems "resolute" in deciding not to bring her the Tsaritsa's slippers, but her "devilish" beauty suggests that his resolve will once again be reversed. Indeed, Oksana almost seems to cast a spell upon the blacksmith. Her "devilish" beauty, we recall, was undermined as "repulsive," and her tresses were likened to snakes. We may also recall that Oksana shrieked when Vacula first surprised her with the mirror (207), just as the witch had shrieked upon "seeing" herself in the dark near the devil. Later, we read that Oksana, unable to sleep, is "tossing in a bewitching nakedness that the nocturnal murkiness concealed even from her herself [*sic*]" (204). A similar murkiness had enveloped Soloha and the devil so that "absolutely nothing could be seen that took place further between them." Here, we read that Oksana "completley burned and by morning was up to her ears in love with the blacksmith." Earlier, her eyes repeatedly "burned." All these details tend to render Oksana strangely witchlike.

Desperate, and still carrying the sack with the devil, Vacula decides to visit Paunchy Patsyuk, a man who reportedly "knows all the devils" (222). Patsyuk proves of little help, but Vacula manages to catch the devil, whom he forces to fly him to the Tsaritsa in St. Petersburg. Once there, Vacula makes the devil shrink himself and crawl into Vacula's pocket. This strangely echoes the devil's capturing the moon and putting it into his own pocket. And the devil's concealment in Vacula's pocket parallels his concealment in a sack. Moreover, the other would-be lovers are confused by various villagers for sackfuls of rewards for singing Christmas carols. The bulging pocket or sack image is thus sustained throughout.

Vacula meets some cossack friends, who escort him to the Tsaritsa. Potyomkin is there, and in a playful twist of the "Potyomkin façade," Vacula mistakes him for the Tsar (236). He then humorously but successfully asks the Tsaritsa for her slippers.

Just as there are perhaps some hints of witchery about Oksana, some rather unlikely parallels may be found between the good blacksmith (who works in fire) and the devil (by whose help he wins the "burning" Oksana). Trying to seduce Soloha, the devil claims he is ready to "throw himself into the water and send his soul straight to hell" (217) if denied her favors. While Vacula is obtaining the slippers to win Oksana, there is a rumor that he has drowned himself (239), but she "knew that the blacksmith was too devout to undertake the destruction of his soul" (240). (It is here that we learn of Oksana's falling in love with him and "completely burning.") Later, Vacula "rewards" the devil with three blows of a long stick; when Vacula comes to ask for Oksana's hand, Chub whips him three times (perhaps as a "reward" for his earlier pummeling) before consenting.

Despite these parallels, Vacula is of course quite "devout," as Oksana puts it. At the end, he paints yet another mural demeaning the devil. And earlier, he seems to capture the devil by making the sign of the cross. The above similarities between Vacula and the devil, like Oksana's witchlike qualities, may therefore be seen to suggest that even people who are happily united and saved in Gogol's world are dangerously close to a quite opposite fate. Goodness and evil seem close to being reversed. (As the story begins, a "good man" is said to pawn his belongings at the tavern, and the devil is first introduced as having "one night left to instruct good people in sin.")

Like goodness and evil, so God and the devil seem dangerously close. "My God," thinks Vacula, why is Oksana so "devilishly" beautiful? (221) And after the devil takes Vacula to St. Petersburg, a cossack asks him why "God" has brought him there. God, we recall, was also wrongly accused of the devil's tamperings with the night. As the reader progresses, it seems an increasingly odd reversal that the devil figures so prominently in a tale called "Christmas Eve."

Notes

1. In "The Sorochintsy Fair," an old woman who discerns the devil in the aspect of a pig is so intoxicated that she walks in circles (I: 123- 4). In "St. John's Eve," some drunks in a tavern perceive that a roast sheep takes on the face of Basavryuk, raises its head, and meaningfully winks at them (151).

2. *Verno* means both "surely" and "truly."

3. Setchkarev, p. 106.

4. In "Rome," an old man who is considering marriage consults a physician concerning how he can fulfill the duties of a husband "with honor" (III:232).

5. Gogol achieves a similar humorous expansion of meaning by referring to the devil and "his moon" (204).

6. Victor Shklovsky, "Art as Technique," in *Russian Formalist Criticism: Four Essays*, trans. Lemon and Reis (Lincoln, Nebraska, 1965), p. 18.

"THE TERRIBLE VENGEANCE"

The cossack Danilo, his wife Katherine, and their two-year-old son arrive at a wedding celebration. A strange cossack appears, who suddenly turns into a hideous old man, recognized as "the sorcerer." He vanishes when icons are turned toward him.

Mountains near the Dnieper River are strangely described. Dead men rise from their graves. Back home, Danilo argues and fights with Katherine's father, who was said to be missing at the wedding. Katherine dreams that her father is the sorcerer and that he incestuously desires her. Danilo spies on Katherine's father and sees him, as the sorcerer, conjure up Katherine's soul. When Danilo returns home, she has apparently dreamed of her soul's recent adventure.

The sorcerer is imprisoned for treachery. Hoping he will repent to save his soul, Katherine sets him free. Polish troops attack. As Danilo fights them, he is killed by the sorcerer. The Dnieper River is strangely described. The sorcerer, conjuring, sees an unfamiliar soul that frightens him. Katherine dreams that her father will kill her son, and he does. A ghostly horseman lurks in the mountains. The Dnieper River is seen to contain the souls of drowned maidens. Katherine, half insance with grief, tries to kill her father, but he kills her. The ghostly horseman appears to the sorcerer, who, strangely terrified, recognizes him as the soul he saw while conjuring. He visits and kills a hermit who refuses to pray for him. The horseman appears, kills the sorcerer, and throws him into an abyss.

From a blind bandora player, we finally learn the story behind all this. Long ago two cossacks, Ivan and Petro, had sworn to share their fortunes equally. When Petro murdered Ivan and his young son, God allowed Ivan to devise a punishment. Petro's descendants are wicked, until the last one does such evil that his ancestors rise in agony from their graves. Petro, however, can only writhe beneath the ground. At the end, Ivan, as a ghostly horseman, throws Petro's last descendant into an abyss, where his ancestors eternally gnaw his bones and he, growing larger, causes the earth to tremble.

In retrospect, we perceive that this background tale is quite literally behind the story proper. Just as the abruptly changing Dnieper

(I:176-77) contains the souls of drowned maidens, mountain tremors include the subterranean writhing of Petro's monstrous bones. Looking back, one realizes that the final legend lurked constantly beneath the surface of the story. A vivid picture of mountains reflected in the Dnieper ("those mountains—are not mountains") furtively hints at Petro's bones. Even the title, which as we progress seems to predict revenge upon the sorcerer, also abruptly expands in meaning when we realize that his evil life is a part of Petro's punishment—that the evil we have (correctly) expected to be avenged is actually a "terrible" element of a very different vengeance.

Supplementing this superimposition of realities, prophetic hints and forward-leaning details occur throughout. Katherine, for example, has three prophetic dreams. In the first, the sorcerer is her father, who reveals his incestuous desire as she stands before him. This prefigures the scene where Danilo watches the sorcerer conjure up Katherine's soul before him in an effort to facilitate possession of her body. Apparently, he can conjure up the souls of people who are asleep, and she is concurrently having her second dream. This dream predicts Katherine's death, but the point is made that she does not "know" all her soul knows. Her third dream, from which she awakes with a scream, reveals that the sorcerer has murdered her child.

Earlier, the child had also awakened with a scream when the corpses first rose from their graves. As Bely has suggested, this scream, which seems to reply to a corpse's, is one of a series of details anticipating the child's death.[1] Katherine wipes the child with a handkerchief embroidered in red (247), and she tells Danilo that if he dies fighting her father, the child may "cry under the knives" of the enemy (252). Also, the child reaches for their friend Gorobets' red pipe. "He'll follow in his father's footsteps," says Gorobets. "Hasn't even left his cradle behind, and he's already thinking of smoking a pipe" (271). As Bely explains, the word *lyul'ka* means both "cradle" and "pipe,"[2] and the red pipe anticipates blood in the cradle: the child reaches for his symbolic death. "Within four lines," Bely concludes, the child has been butchered.[3] The words "he'll follow in his father's footsteps" (not mentioned by Bely) are also ironically prophetic, for the sorcerer has just killed the child's father.

We may also add to Bely's findings that Danilo, sensing that his own death is near, tells Katherine: "don't leave our son when I'm gone" (265). After this, the sorcerer kills the boy and then Katherine. She thus seems to comply most ironically with Danilo's wish.[4] The idea is further stressed by Danilo's dying words: "tell Katherine not to abandon my son!" (267).

In the final background tale, Petro murders both Ivan and his little son.[5] We therefore encounter the murders of two children late in the story. When the sorcerer first appeared at the wedding, we had read: " 'The sorcerer has appeared again!' cried the mothers, seizing their children in their arms." Soon after, Katherine had related a rumor that the sorcerer was ugly when he was born: no small child wanted to play with him. In context, these details tend to anticipate the two child murders. However, since the "actual" chronology is quite different from the narrational chronology, the sequence forms a strangely circular pattern.

Bely has aptly connected the sorcerer's fiery eyes and red jacket with various images of sparks, pipe coals, and blood throughout the story.[6] In addition, we may note that Danilo dips his red jacket sleeve in the water while returning home by boat (246). This dripping red sleeve prefigures his fight with the sorcerer, wherein we see that "crimson blood" stains the "sleeve" of Danilo's jacket (252). Similarly, Danilo's "red cap," so conspicuous in battle with the Poles, may suggest his impending death. Earlier, Danilo says that he had removed the hat of a Tartar "together with his head" (249). Still another Gogolian connection between clothes and the person wearing them occurs when Katherine's father turns into the sorcerer. Watching him, Danilo first observes a change in his clothing and only later, in his face.

After dreaming of her father's incestuous desire, Katherine says to Danilo, who is leaving: "Lock me in the room, and take the key with you." Later, Danilo fails to take the key to the sorcerer's cell with him, and Katherine uses it to release her father, who then commits four murders. He persuades her to release him "for the sake of " her "unfortunate mother," an idea which she repeats. He had murdered her mother, and soon he murders her.

As Bely has illustrated in detail, "The Terrible Vengeance" is an "apotheosis" of the word "not" (*ne*), and negation especially often attends the sorcerer.[7] At the opening marriage celebration, the guests marvel at Katherine's beauty, "but they marveled still more that her old father had not come with her." He had been away in foreign lands and could surely have told many fascinating stories. "Everything is not the same there: the people are not the same, they have no Christian churches. . . . But he had not come." So ends the first paragraph, with an abrupt return from a rambling digression. Actually, although the mention of "no Christian churches" seems to lead nowhere, Danilo will later decide that Katherine's father is the antichrist (260).[8]

This idea is developed by icons. Gorobets, the host, has some special icons which protect their owner from "unclean forces." When he brings them out to bless the wedding couple, a cossack guest is transformed into a hideous old man. (He is repeatedly termed "the cossack" even as he undergoes this transformation.) Before Katherine's father is thought to be the anti-christ, he sits "opposite" the icons at Danilo's (254). (The word "opposite," *protiv*, also means "against, in opposition to.") And as mentioned above, the sorcerer vanishes from the wedding when the special icons are turned toward him.

False focus in the story becomes complex even for Gogol. "The cossack" is really "the sorcerer," who is really "Katherine's father," who is really the last, and most evil, descendant of Petro. The mountains are really the reflections of mountains, which really include a sinister dimension of writhing swollen bones. When Danilo watches the sorcerer conjuring, he first sees "something white, like a cloud." He then observes that "the cloud was not a cloud," but an airy woman. Then he realizes: "it is Katherine!" Finally, we learn that the cloud which was an airy woman who is Katherine is really Katherine's soul.

Danilo's first glimpse through the sorcerer's window reveals mystic symbols on the walls and bats flitting about the room, casting shadows upon the walls, door, and floor. As the sorcerer begins conjuring: "the symbols began to change more quickly on the wall, and the bats began flying more swiftly, up and down, back and forth." Although the symbols had not been described as "changing" before, their sudden acceleration seems strangely justified by the acceleration of bat shadows, also changing upon the walls. Here we have an especially convincing instance of the Gogolian technique of introducing as "increased" a previously unmentioned condition.

As suggested above, nature in "The Terrible Vengeance" seems to conceal a second level of reality. Just as "those mountains—are not mountains," but Petro's rumbling, swollen bones, the "wondrous" yet abruptly "terrifying" Dnieper River conceals the ghostly bodies of drowned maidens. Its waters "dismally" murmur as Katherine first passes by her imprisoned father (261). And the Dnieper seems to await Katherine's body, as both she and Danilo separately suggest (252,264). We were also told, early in the story, that "those woods, standing on the hills, are not woods. . . ." Climbing a tree to watch the sorcerer (conjure up Katherine's soul), Danilo hears a sound as if the evening wind "was bending the silvery willows still lower into the water." [9] In Bely's view, "Katherine's soul is like a dryad (the soul of trees)." [10]

Tree descriptions also precede the deaths of both Danilo and the sorcerer. When the Polish soldiers arrive, they are said to cover the hill like leaves, fallen from a tree in autumn (266). And as the ghostly horseman pursues the sorcerer, trees seem to surround him, as though alive, trying to strangle him (276). Thus, the phrase "those trees are not trees" expands in meaning beyond the idea of reflection in the water, as did the similar negation of mountains.

The third aspect of nature that a Dnieper view seems to negate is the nearby fields ("those meadows—are not meadows"). From their boat on the river, Katherine and Danilo soon watch corpses rise from their graves in a nearby cemetery.

The story draws deeply upon folklore, both for content and style,[11] which allows Gogol to presume that nature shares the feelings of his characters. A rainy morning, for example, parallels Katherine's sad awakening, as Bely has shown.[12] To such "natural" pathetic fallacies Gogol then adds his own sinister prophetic twists, as we have seen. Other elements of the story taken from folklore are a powerful sleeping horseman, a lament by the widow of a warrior, and even the notion of "intoxicating" the enemy by "treating" them to a barrage of fire. For instance, Danilo speaks of "treating" Polish soldiers to "lead plums" (253).

Danilo's death may be seen as the central tragedy of the story, for it also seems to doom his wife and son, as Katherine has predicted (252). His death is described in two ways, both traditional in folklore. Danilo is said to be "asleep, not to awaken" and to be lying drunk, "not to become sober for a long time." Earlier, he had twice become upset that the sorcerer refused to drink with him. The sorcerer's murdering Danilo "into drunkenness" thus seems oddly logical. Somewhat similarly, Danilo's "sleeping" death seems appropriately followed by two descriptions of the sleeping horseman, who in a sense avenges Danilo's death.

The sorcerer visits a hermit, who lives in a cave and sleeps in a coffin instead of a bed. Asked by the sorcerer to pray for him, the hermit refuses, saying: "It is not good for the man who is with you!" (277). Enraged, the sorcerer kills him. The man's coffin, previously focused, may be seen to anticipate his death.

"The Terrible Vengeance" richly exemplifies Gogol's "already" *(uzhe)* device, which tends to create the impression that we blinked our eyes and missed something. For example, the sorcerer seems about to discover Danilo, who has climbed a tree to spy on him through the window. Realizing this danger, Katherine's soul shudders: "But already Danilo had been on the ground for some time and was making his way. . . ." (259). Other examples are Katherine's words to her father when he has "already" disappeared (after she has set him free, as he hastens to escape), the cossacks' pursuit of the sorcerer (who has just murdered Katherine) when he has "already" disappeared, and the last paragraph of the story, which begins: "Already the blind man had finished his song; already he had started to pluck the strings once again; already he had started singing. . . ." [13]

Gogol also typically uses reversal words and syllogistic narration. For example, the sorcerer tells Danilo: "I shoot poorly: my bullets only pierce the heart at two hundred yards." [14] When Katherine first passes her imprisoned father, we are led to believe: (1) that no one is coming, (2) that she has come, and (3) that it is only a cossack. She then (1) does appear, (2) leaves when he begs her to help him, and (3) returns to set him free.

Gogol also tinges point of view with eeriness when fright is described. Pursued by the horseman, the sorcerer turns wildly around but still feels that he is headed toward his enemy. "Not a single person in the world" could tell what he felt. "There is not such a word in the world, with which it could be described." Killed, the sorcerer opens his eyes. "But he was already a dead man and gazed like a dead man." His bones are then gnawed in a chasm "which not one person has yet seen."

These weird insights intensify repeated hints that the characters sense the supernatural forces around them. Katherine does not know all that her soul knows. The sorcerer, ignorant of the background story "explaining" his evil life, is strangely terrified by the unfamiliar face that appears to him in his conjuring. And when this face reappears to kill him: "He himself could not understand why he became so totally flustered. . . ." At the very end, when the reader learns the background story, these descriptions seem strangely justified.

Throughout "The Terrible Vengeance," we encounter unsettling hints of another reality. Gogol's use of forward-leaning details and prophetic dreams seems especially effective. His use of negation also questions surface appearances. Perhaps strangest of all, even the final background story seems to prefigure itself. As it begins, Petro declares: "Look, Ivan, whatever you obtain, all will be shared equally: when one of us has happiness—happiness to the other; when one has sorrow—sorrow to both; when one has booty—the booty will be shared equally . . ." (279). While hardly apparent in context, Ivan will later follow Petro's proposal by devising the latter's punishment, thus sharing sorrow in a way quite unintended by Petro. This sorrow, of course, becomes (has already become) the story proper.

Notes

1. Belyj, *Masterstvo Gogolya,* p. 64.

2. Belyj, *Masterstvo Gogolya,* pp. 58, 64.

3. Belyj, *Masterstvo Gogolya,* p. 64.

4. Such phrasing often occurs when two realities seem to overlap. See especially "May Night . . ."

5. Belyj imaginatively connects this with the murder of Ivas by Petrus in "St. John's Eve." *Masterstvo Gogolya,* p. 69.

6. See especially *ibid.,* pp. 65-66.

7. Belyj, *Masterstvo Gogolya,* p. 66.

8. Belyj relates the word "antichrist" to the general theme of negation.

9. Once again, Gogol increases a previously unmentioned state of being ("still lower"). See also pp. 246, 248, 255.

10. Belyj, *Masterstvo Gogolya,* p. 63.

11. See Setchkarev, p. 111.

12. Belyj, *Lug zelyonyj,* p. 120. Gogol, I:159.

13. For three more uses of the *uzhe* device, see III:247, 258.

14. He similarly describes his swordsmanship.

"IVAN FYODOROVICH SHPONKA AND HIS AUNT"

The beginning features a pun: "With this story there happened a story. . . ." (The Russian *istoriya,* "story," can also mean "an unpleasant event.") As Panko soon explains, his illiterate wife lined her baking pan with the pages comprising the last half of the story. And since a friend in Gadyach had written down the story (because of Panko's "sievelike" memory), it must be printed "without an ending." Thus, the reader understands the opening pun: the tale has lost its tail. And so, when we eventually find that the last words of "Shponka" refer to "the next chapter," we smile, knowingly, at Gogol's little joke. But it may not be quite that simple.

In the first place, this playfully forward-leaning ending is preceded by a series of strangely prophetic details. Panko tells us in his introduction that once, when he chanced to travel through Gadyach, he tied a knot in his handkerchief, "promising himself " to ask his friend about the (written-down) ending if he sneezed: "But all in vain." The reader concludes that Panko did not sneeze. But as he (syllogistically) explains, he did sneeze, did use the handkerchief, but forgot anyway. (This, however, was anticipated by the mention of Panko's "sievelike" memory.)

If the reader is curious, he has only to ask the friend in Gadyach, who "will tell it with the great pleasure, even, perhaps, from beginning to end once again." This friend can easily be recognized by the way he "always swings his arms." As the local assessor used to say: "Look, look, there goes a windmill!"

Part One begins with Shponka's boyhood and presents "a certain occurrence which influenced his entire life" (I:285). As class prefect, the lad was bribed with a sumptuous pancake and caught by the teacher, who "seized him by the ear," dragging him to the center of the room. As explained in context, the incident may have dissuaded him from a civil service career, where "one cannot always cover one's tracks." Shponka's life as an officer seems humorously uneventful. His only intriguing habit is to consult his fortune-telling book, and even this he does quite mechanically.

In Part Two, Shponka travels home with his fortune-telling book to take over management of his estate from Aunt Vasilisa. On the way he meets Storchenko, a dynamic neighboring landowner who plugs up his ears at night because a cockroach once crawled into his left ear. When Shponka arrives at his estate, the first thing he sees is a windmill. Apparently from the excitement of homecoming, Shponka's heart begins to beat strongly when the windmill has "looked out" and "waved its wings." This nearly alive windmill may remind the reader of the windmill-like storyteller in Gadyach, who knows the lost ending. Finally, Shponka is met by his masculine aunt and the house serfs, including two servant girls "in woolen shifts."

Part Three, entitled "Auntie," points out "nature's unforgivable mistake"—having her wear women's clothes when she should have sported jackboots and a moustache. Before long, she calls her nephew's attention to some rich neighboring land, claiming it is really his. Storchenko, she says, may have the deed that proves this.

In Part Four, Shponka visits Storchenko and asks about the deed. Obviously disturbed, Storchenko claims to have trouble hearing and quickly retells the story of the cockroach in his left ear. Shponka somehow persists, but his host denies that there ever was a deed. While they are talking, Storchenko suddenly notes that his "mother and sisters" are approaching. "Consequently, dinner is ready." A few lines later, we learn that his mother is "a perfect coffeepot in a little cap." The faint, suggestive relationship between "coffeepot" and "dinner" may be seen (with Gogolian precarious logic) to expand quite remarkably the meaning of "consequently."

Part Five, the "last" part, is entitled "Auntie's New Plan." Shponka relates his failure to find the deed, blushingly noting that one of Storchenko's sisters is especially beautiful. "A new idea," we read, "flashed through" the aunt's head. It may have been "preordained," she declares, that Shponka should marry this girl. Together they drive to Storchenko's, where the aunt arranges for Shponka and the chosen sister to be alone. But their conversation is meager indeed.

Shponka's famous words ("There are many flies in summer, Miss"), which are all he can muster during the fifteen minutes he is expected to propose marriage, seem strangely appropriate. For as Shponka stresses the multiplicity of flies, he may well be uneasy about the prospect of multiplying his own species. (Soon after this, he exclaims in terror that he would have no idea "what to do" with a wife.) In *Dead Souls,* as Proffer has observed, an extended pattern of interlocking details likens men to flies and women to pieces of sugar.[1] The more one ponders these associations, the more alien and uneasy Gogol's humor becomes.

On their way home, the aunt terrifies Shponka with the news that Storchenko's mother has already agreed to have him as a son-in-law. Shponka retires "earlier than usual" and has a grotesque nightmare, which his fortune-telling book seems helpless to decipher.

Shponka's dream first shows him running and running . . . "Suddenly, someone seized him by the ear" (as did his teacher, in the "occurrence which influenced his entire life"). Here, it is his wife. Next, goose-faced wives close in from all sides. His face perspiring, Shponka reaches for his handkerchief (as did our narrator). But the action fails (as with the narrator), for: "there was a wife in his pocket, too." Now he removes some cotton stuffing from his ear (an echo of Storchenko) and—"a wife was there as well."

Told twice, Storchenko's cockroach story uneasily anticipates the wife in Shponka's ear. The "pillows" of Storchenko's cheeks, as kissed by Shponka in greeting, are also noted twice (when they first meet and when Shponka visits him about the deed). The word *podushki,* "pillows," literally suggests "under the ears," so it refers to "cheeks" with Gogolian precarious logic. The pun, moreover, reinforces the focus upon Storchenko's ears.

As the dream continues, sexual images take over. Shponka suddenly hops on one leg, which his aunt says he must do now because he is married. He then approaches "auntie, who was no longer auntie, but a belfry." Shponka, his wife informs him, is "a bell," and therefore she is "pulling" him.

Finally he dreams that "his wife was not a person at all, but some kind of woolen material." (Here we may recall the two servant girls "in woolen shifts.") The "wife" is measured and cut by a merchant, but the tailor deems her "bad material." Colloquially, the adjective used here for "bad" *(durnaya)* means "venereal" when applied to "disease." Further dark humor results from the idea of a wife as a piece of woolen material, measured and cut, which seems quite appropriate to evoke Shponka's fearful picture of what a wife might be like. "I wouldn't know at all what to do with her!" he has exclaimed (306), and this presumably results in his dreaming the material "bad." And his dream notion that a female (seen as a flat woolen area) is "not a person at all" is perhaps even more darkly humorous.[2]

Though composed from fragments of the past, Shponka's dream reveals fears of a future marriage that may well take place. Time is thus doubly dissolved, as if seen from some unearthly perspective, and perhaps one recalls the aunt's idea that Shponka's marriage may have been "preordained" (303). Literally, *na rodu napisano* ("preordained") reads: "written on the family" (kin, origin, birth).

Shponka's birth is a tricky question, but it seems reasonably obvious that he is a blood relation of Storchenko. Suggesting that the rich neighboring land is really Shponka's, the aunt asks: "Do you remember Stepan Kuzmich? What am I saying: remember! You were so little then, you couldn't even pronounce his name. . . . He, I must inform you, began to visit your mother when you were not yet in the world; true, at times when your father was not at home" (295). Here, Gogol has the aunt casually focus on Stepan's name just as we learn that Shponka should perhaps be thought of as Ivan *Stepanovich* ("son of Stepan"). Note also the false focus of "your father."

The aunt goes on to reveal that Stepan Kuzmich supposedly deeded the land to Shponka as a gift, but his mother, whom the "devil himself" could not understand, put it "God knows where." The aunt thinks that Storchenko has it: he inherited the entire estate. The exact relationship of Shponka to Storchenko's sister is thus unclear,[3] but the aunt's idea that their marriage may be "written on the family" acquires considerable irony.[4]

It now seems clear that Shponka's maternal aunt (287) has called him home to recover the land that is "rightfully" his. Her letter suggesting that he retire maintains she is too old to look after things (287), but this is obviously untrue. To Shponka's astonishment, she almost hoists him up in her arms when he arrives. Rather, she wishes to increase the lands under her own management. Her scheme, then, may well be to have Shponka marry into his own family to obtain, for her, his own land.

In her letter, the aunt mentions that she wishes to discuss some "business" with Shponka. After his arrival, she announces her desire to discuss some "business" that has been occupying her. She begins by mentioning the number of serfs in his village, then uses her favorite phrase: "But that's not the point" (295; literally: "But not about that is the business"). Next, she focuses upon the rich neighboring land, revealing that the size of Shponka's estate was precisely "the point" after all.

Similarly, "Auntie's New Plan" (the title of Chapter Five) is really the same old "business" in disguise: when Storchenko denies knowledge of the deed, she decides to increase her holdings through the dowry that Shponka will receive. (She is even prepared to take Storchenko to court if he refuses to provide a dowry.) Her new idea is therefore really the old one—a typical Gogolian false focus. And the aunt's "entirely new plan," which, according to the last sentence of the story, is revealed in the "next chapter," is almost surely just another scheme to bully Shponka into marriage.

Finally, if Shponka's dream is construed as a Gogolian prophetic nightmare,[5] he does eventually marry Storchenko's sister—with some rather startling and uncomfortable results. In this sense, the ending of "Shponka" may be projected from the surviving text, and the final irony is that the "loss" of the "real" ending matters little. (If we recall that the seizing of Shponka's ear by a teacher was said to have "influenced his entire life," and that his "wife" also seizes his ear as the dream begins, this hidden projection of Shponka's married life seems even more likely.)

A ghostly projection of Shponka's (incestuous? and therefore doubly unpleasant?) married life, then, may even be anticipated by the opening sentence: "With this story there happened a story." For then, the "unpleasant story" becomes not only the loss of the ending, but also the (projected) lost ending itself—Shponka's married life. It even seems possible that the dramatic appearance of the windmill (when Shponka arrives home) signals a "retelling" (mentioned earlier) of his story from "beginning" (the revelation of his birth) to "end" (the projected marriage). And all this was perhaps "preordained" (written on the family), which may explain Shponka's oddly mechanical attachment to his fortune-telling book. Yet he cannot discern his future in the book, for he consults it "because he liked to encounter something familiar there, something read several times already" (288). In this sense, the story features the Gogolian notion that if we look more closely, or somewhat differently, at reality, we may well see across the apparent temporal and spatial barriers of "this world." [6]

"Shponka," then, may be considered an abrupt reversal of the hero's life that includes, however, a Gogolian haunting return (when Shponka marries back into his "own" family). Other reversals tend to reinforce this basic one: the aunt has apparently been given the wrong sex, Panko seems to be reminded by a fat peasant woman that his friend in Gadyach is a bachelor, and so on.[7]

Notes

1. Proffer, pp. 85-86.

2. In *The Marriage,* the process of finding a husband is amusingly confused with selling wool.

When Shponka first mentions the girl whose beauty has impressed him, the aunt asks what sort of dress she had on, quickly mentioning that "now it is difficult to find such strong material" as her housecoat is made of.

3. Yet another clue may be that Storchenko's mother "seems" to stare "fixedly" at Shponka when he and she are introduced (298).

4. In "The Terrible Vengeance," Ivan prefaces his punishment by noting that Petro has deprived him of descendants by killing his son: "And a person without an honorable line and without descendants is like a bread seed, thrown into the ground and vanishing uselessly in the ground." Answering his aunt's letter, Shponka declares that he was unable "to fulfill" her *former* request "about the wheat seeds." (Everything else in his letter directly answers the only letter of his aunt's which we read.) Shponka's strangely stressed inability to bring wheat seeds home possibly anticipates his inability to propose marriage after his arrival there, and perhaps even his inability to sow seeds of his own (if indeed his aunt's schemes are eventually successful) in the sense of the "bread seed" mentioned by Ivan. The bachelor in the introduction to "Shponka," we recall, resembled a windmill. Windmills grind up seeds. In Part Three, the aunt is seen to have "a miller" in her power, except that he has still not married her. If these details are united by Gogolian precarious logic, Shponka's seeing the windmill first upon his arrival home may suggest the futility of his own marriage, even if it later takes place.

5. See especially "The Terrible Vengeance" and *The Government Inspector.*

6. In addition to the dream, there is a fragment of conscious "reality"

which seems teasingly prophetic. This is the scene wherein Shponka is left alone with Storchenko's sister (and speaks only about the flies in summer).

> The fair young lady remained and sat down on the sofa. Ivan Fyodorovich was sitting on his chair as on needles, turning red and lowering his eyes; but the young lady, it seemed, did not notice this at all and kept indifferently sitting on the sofa, diligently examining the windows and walls or following with her eyes a cat which had timorously run past beneath the chairs. (305)

This passage may perhaps also be taken as a faint foreglimpse of the couple's (projected) married life. Gogol used a cat to portend disaster much more obviously in "Old World Landowners." Here, the timorous cat seems identified with Shponka's uneasy fears and his desire to escape.

7. When the aunt tries to convince Shponka that he should marry, she says he is "almost thirty-eight" and that "it's time to think about children!" (306). He seems both frightened and confused, whereupon she declares that he is still "just a little child" and so could not be expected to know about such things. At Storchenko's, a friend asserts that his turkeys are "so plump" it is "even repulsive to see" when they walk about his yard (299-300).

"THE ENCHANTED PLACE"

Despite its obvious nonsense, this little story subtly blends at least two realities. In Setchkarev's view, it draws its effects from a constant swing back and forth "between the supernatural and inexplicable to prosaic reality." [1] Since this begins with the abrupt transformation of a small plot of ground, the "enchanted place" quite literally superimposes two realities. As the tale progresses, we realize that "the place" is "two places." The enchanted place is a capricious stepping stone between two realities, each of which normally shuts out the other—at least with respect to human vision.

The story is built upon a sequence of Gogolian reversals and ironic juxtapositions which reinforce the effect of parallel and slightly overlapping realities. The sacristan opens with an exclamation about God that introduces the topic of the Unclean Spirit. This uneasy juxtaposition is immediately reiterated: "if a devilish force feels like hoodwinking, it will hoodwink; my god, it will hoodwink!" The sacristan then lapses into what seems a nonsensical recollection.

> I was no more than about eleven; well, no, not eleven: I remember like now that once I was starting to run around on all fours, barking like a dog, when dad yelled at me, shaking his head: "Hey, Foma, Foma! It's time for you to be getting married, and you're stupid as a young mule!"

Most readers will probably find themselves twisted syllogistically. Foma seems: (1) about eleven, (2) much less, and (3) considerably more, but acting less. "Grandfather was still alive then," the sacristan continues, "and on his legs—may he hiccup lightly in the other world—quite sturdy." This broken wording allows a Gogolian glimpse of "the other world" within the (verbal) texture of the "real" one. (Focus is typically on a man now dead.) Moreover, the phrase pertaining to the next world prophetically interrupts the hero's sturdiness on his legs. For the grandfather soon begins to dance wildly, and his legs suddenly refuse to be lifted, as if turned to wood (I:311). He has been dancing at the enchanted place, which he angrily calls "a devilish place," adding hopes that Satan will "choke on a rotten melon." At this point, the place abruptly alters in the grandfather's perception, and the devil apparently "hoodwinks" him into a useless search for buried treasure.

Dancing, especially by older people, is tinged with eeriness in *Evenings*,[2] and the foreshadowing of devilish woodenness by "broken" sturdiness seems quite in keeping with the Dikanka world. Here, the connection is reinforced by the grandfather's exclamation: "Dance, dog's children!" which he utters, just before dancing himself, to his grandchildren, including our narrator, who had wanted to "run about on all fours, barking like a dog."

The occasion for all this dancing is that merchant friends have stopped by for the evening and are eating melons. (The sacristan's family lived by trading melons and other crops [3] to merchants for chickens, eggs, etc.) Grandfather and the merchants greatly enjoy their melons, which the reader may connect with the grandfather's apparently disastrous oath about Satan choking on a rotten melon. Melons, as we shall see, figure in the story suspiciously often. At the end, for example, we are told that rich harvests were later reaped in this region, except for the enchanted place. Its bad crops include "watermelon that is not watermelon . . . the devil knows what!" (316). The story thus ends with perhaps a final result of hoping the devil will choke on a rotten melon. (Also, we may note, it ends with the devil after opening with a reference to God.)

In all, the grandfather seems to visit the enchanted place three times, yet it can be said that the only time he "goes there" (the second) is the only time he fails to arrive. The first time, the place abruptly changes, and he seems to find himself near some neighbors' lands: at "a place, it seemed, not entirely unfamiliar" (311). Apparently seeing the priest's pigeonhouse and the clerk's barn, he presumes himself transplanted to a different place within his own reality. But it gradually seems more likely that he has been shifted to another reality while "staying" at the same (enchanted) place.

Deciding that there is buried treasure nearby, the grandfather is about "to spit on his hands in order to dig" when he remembers he has no tools with him. "There's nothing to do," he concludes, "except mark the place, at least, in order not to forget later!" (312). If indeed this is a different reality, we have here the joke about marking an "X" on the side of one's boat to locate a good fishing spot, but

with a Gogolian twist. This fisherman, we could say, is in a different
lake, and "marking the place" will anyway be futile. Nevertheless,
the grandfather places a broken branch on a nearby grave and
somehow wanders home.

The next day, with tools for digging, grandfather tries to return to
where he thought he had been taken. He is unsuccessful, however, in
reproducing the relationship between pigeon-house and barn. "This
is not the place," he concludes, which seems to be correct in a way he
does not intend. His reference is to landmarks in what is presumably
the wrong "reality." A light rain begins, "as if on purpose" (313).
Grandfather curses once again, this time hoping Satan will not live
to see his children. The rain immediately comes down in torrents.

Returning home, grandfather scares the sacristan's little brother,
threatening to trade him "instead of a watermelon" to the merchants for chickens. He also gives the children a strangely shaped
melon "with three coils, like a snake." All this seems to interconnect
the grandfather's two oaths about Satan (melon and children)
rather ominously. And the snakelike melon with three coils may
even be seen to anticipate the melons which are not melons at the
end of the story.

That evening, grandfather begins his third (and apparently second authentic) visit by cursing the enchanted place and hitting it
with a spade. Once again, the scenery instantly alters, and he recognizes the grave with its broken branch. "If only I don't make a
mistake," he thinks. These words of course refer to digging in the
"wrong" place, but the grandfather's "mistake" will be his digging
up a worthless treasure in the "right" place.

With great effort, grandfather pries away a stone lying on the
grave, and we read: "Now, things will go more lively" (313-14).
Grandfather then takes out some tobacco and is raising it to his nose
when "something sneezes so lustily that the trees shake and his
"whole face" is splattered. No one is in sight. "No, it can be seen that
the devil does not like tobacco," he concludes. (Gogol typically
employs *vidno*, "it can be seen," in the sense of "apparently" just
when nothing can be seen. In "The Overcoat," a supposed ghost
sneezes from tobacco, besplattering the eyes of three people, because
the tobacco was of a kind which "surely" [*verno*] even a corpse cannot
endure [III:170].)

Grandfather digs, mocked by various birds and animals, who seem to repeat his exclamations. Finally he strikes an old cauldron, which he presumes contains treasure. Wishing to sniff tobacco again, he reconsiders, because Satan "will spit in" his eyes once more.

Carrying home the cauldron, grandfather is taken for a reveling villager and doused with hot dishwater by the sacristan's mother. "Devil's woman!" grandfather exclaims, wiping his head, which is covered with "melon and watermelon peelings." Once again, he seems to suffer from his wish that the devil will choke on a rotten melon. Presumably unaware of such a cause, grandfather is nevertheless convinced that "if the devil feels like hoodwinking," he will do so: the cauldron contains not treasure, but rubbish. Gogol has the sacristan twice mention "gold" before revealing this. And from that time on, we read, grandfather admonished the children never to trust the devil. He thus strikes a final note similar to that in the ending of "Nevsky Prospect," which street, illuminated by Satan, is also not to be trusted.

Notes

1. Setchkarev, p. 117.

2. See especially "The Sorochintsy Fair."

3. Gogol puns on these crops by having the grandfather termed "the horseradish" (something like "the old geezer") while he dances alongside the cucumber beds (311).

CHAPTER 3

Mirgorod

"OLD WORLD LANDOWNERS"

Two elderly landowners, Pulheria Ivanovna and Afanasy Ivanovich, live quietly on their small estate. Afanasy Ivanovich loves to eat and tease his wife. One day Pulheria Ivanovna's gray cat runs away to live with wild tomcats. She returns, then leaves again; Pulheria Ivanovna is convinced that this signifies her own imminent death. She dies. Several years later, one quiet cloudless day, Afanasy Ivanovich thinks he hears Pulheria Ivanovna calling him in the garden. He dies. A distant relative inherits the estate and continues its deterioration with unsuccessful agricultural reforms.

This simple plot gradually develops eerie complexity. Early in the story, Gogol's narrator describes the many servant girls

who for the most part kept running off to the kitchen and sleeping. Pulheria Ivanovna deemed it essential to keep them in the house and strictly watched over their morals. But to her extreme amazement, hardly a few months would pass without the figure of one of the girls becoming much fuller than usual.

67

It seemed even more amazing since in the house there were
almost no single people, excepting only the house boy, who
went about in a long gray jacket, barefooted, and if he was not
eating, then he was surely sleeping. (II:18-19)

As often happens with Gogol, the words suggest a surface picture
which almost obscures a quite different one. The "kitchen," to
which the girls keep running off and sleeping, seems almost to
double as a bedroom. Pulheria Ivanovna's "strict" vigilance seems
almost to reverse itself as the apparent pregnancies are revealed.[1]
And though the house boy's age is not given, his habits of eating and
sleeping create a suggestive, haunting return to the "kitchen." Note
also the repeated indirect association of food and sex.

The coachman, we soon learn, was eternally distilling vodka
under a tree. He would usually begin blabbing such nonsense,
however, that Pulheria Ivanovna would send him off "to the kitchen
to sleep." She thus sends the coachman to the girls over whom she so
"strictly" watches. Later, we read that Pulheria Ivanovna always
persuaded guests to spend the night. "Besides," she would say, "your
coachman, I know your coachman . . . he's already been wetting his
whistle, surely, and by now he's sleeping somewhere" (25).

While all this goes on in the "kitchen," the entire household
indulges in orgies of eating. The serf girls, we learn, used to sneak
into the pantry and overeat "so horribly" that "for a whole day they
would groan and complain about their bellies" (19-20). Afanasy
Ivanovich, who overeats prodigiously, also complains of his "belly,"
the pain of which he improbably cures by additional eating. After
this, his stomach seems to feel "better" (literally, the word means
"lighter," a reversal pun). Later, the tomcats who seduce Pulheria
Ivanovna's gray cat are described as stealing lard from the kitchen
window during the cook's absence (29). The kitchen theme of furtive
food and furtive sex even involves the cats.

These tomcats, we read, finally enticed Pulheria Ivanovna's gray
cat away "like a squad of soldiers entices a stupid peasant girl" (29).
Since Pulheria Ivanovna connects the gray cat with her impending
death, we may note that Afanasy Ivanovich had been an army
officer who "even quite skillfully carried off Pulheria Ivanovna"
when her parents objected to their marrying (16). The human and

feline worlds thus seem even more closely paralleled. In addition, Pulheria Ivanovna feeds her gray cat upon its return, and it "grew fat almost before her eyes" (30). After this, the cat runs away again, and we are told that Pulheria Ivanovna "grew noticeably thinner."

This suggestive cat-human symmetry seems the more eerie because Pulheria Ivanovna, convinced that her death was signaled by the brief return of her gray cat, insists on being buried in her gray dress (30). "God knows what you are saying," Afanasy Ivanovich replies. He goes on to say that such talk frightens him, which reverses the usual pattern: Pulheria Ivanovna, we have seen, says that she becomes frightened when Afanasy Ivanovich teases her, even though she knows he is only joking (26). And well she might: Afanasy Ivanovich's "teasings" seem to have almost sinister results. Before the gray cat leaves, for instance, he pretends that dogs are better than cats. "Be still," says she, ". . . a cat is a quiet creature: it won't do evil to anyone" (28).

Afanasy Ivanovich teases Pulheria Ivanovna by saying that he may "go off to war" (25). She becomes strangely terrified. As seen above the tomcats who seduce her cat are likened to "a squad of soldiers."

To appreciate fully the first way in which Afanasy Ivanovich teases Pulheria Ivanovna, we must return to the first sentence of the story. In an extended comparison, the narrator likens old world landowners to "feeble picturesque houses." This idea of "human houses" recurs throughout the story [2] until at the end, when both landowners have died, we see that the peasants' huts on their property, "which were almost lying on the ground, fell apart entirely." [3] As for the landowners' house, its "most remarkable" feature is its "singing doors. As soon as morning arrived, the singing of the doors would resound throughout the entire house" (17). Four pages later, the parallel becomes quite explicit: "As soon as dawn arrived (they got up early) and as soon as the doors began their discordant concert, they were already sitting at the little table and drinking coffee." This strangely human house even seems to awaken and start the day with its owners. Turning to Afanasy Ivanovich's first "joke," we find: "suppose our house burned down, where would we move to then?" (24). It now appears that this playful question prefigures both the deterioration of the estate and the deaths of its owners. If so, the playful question of where they would "move to" enlarges considerably in meaning. Afanasy Ivanovich used to tease Pulheria Ivanovna with this question, moreover, when "the weather was clear." Later, she seems to call him to his death on a bright clear day; this weather condition is stressed at length by the narrator (37).

But who is this narrator? Just before introducing Afanasy Ivanovich, he casually digresses about two old people "who, alas! are already gone now" and whose estate contains a heap of huts that have fallen apart. He also pictures the place where their house "was standing—and nothing more" (14). The narrator adds that he feels "sad in advance," which apparently refers to his possibly revisiting this estate. "But let us turn to the story," he concludes. In retrospect, however, it seems that the narrator has just prefigured much of the story that follows.

Who is this narrator? He begins his first, second, and fourth sentences with the word "I." "I very much love the modest life of those solitary owners of remote villages . . ." is his beginning, which the third sentence continues:

> The life of their modest owners is so quiet, so quiet, that for a minute one becomes lost in thought and imagines that the passions, desires, and restless creations of the evil spirit that trouble the world do not exist at all, and that you have seen them only in some shining, glittering dream.

In sum: their life is "so quiet, so quiet" that it seems safe from the "evil spirit." Pulheria Ivanovna's death, we recall, is prefigured by her own words: "a cat is a *quiet* creature: it won't do *evil* to anyone" (my emphasis). Afanasy Ivanovich's death, speaking with Pulheria Ivanovna's voice, seems to call him when: "The day was *quiet,* and the sun was *shining*" (37; my emphasis). From the very beginning, then, both deaths seem to be present, "so quiet, so quiet," in "some shining, glittering dream." It only remains for the narrator, gradually, to reveal this. And as he does, his initial focusing upon the "life," the "modest life" of these landowners gradually reverses itself as a focusing upon their ominously developing death. Leading up to the gray coat episode and Pulheria Ivanovna's death, the narrator warns us that a sad event will soon change forever "the life" of that "peaceful little corner" (27).

Five years after Pulheria Ivanovna's death, our narrator visits Afanasy Ivanovich and finds "an old man already without feeling" (36). "But which is stronger in us," he wonders, "passion or habit?" And he (reversely) concludes that "all our passions seemed childish" compared to the old man's "long, slow, almost feelingless habit." Who, one wonders, could have such an insight? Earlier, we recall, the narrator casually mentioned "the passions, desires and restless creations of the evil spirit that trouble the world."

Our narrator seems to have a rather unusual perspective on human passions and habit, on human life and death. Describing the quiet, clear day when Afanasy Ivanovich seems to hear Pulheria Ivanovna calling him, the narrator remarks: "You, without doubt, have sometime chanced to hear a voice, calling you by name, which the common people explain as a soul pining for a person and summoning him, and which is followed inevitably by death. I confess, I was always terrified by that mysterious call" (37). In other words, our narrator was "always" terrified by a call which is followed inevitably by death. And we, "without doubt," have "chanced" to hear it too. "I remember that in childhood," he continues, "I often heard it. . . . At that time the day was usually the most clear and sunny . . . the quiet was deathly . . . not a soul in the garden . . . that terrible quiet in the midst of a cloudless day." The words "deathly" and "soul" are both Gogolian eerie puns. Taken literally, "not a soul" seems to deny the belief that "a soul" is pining for and calling to a living person. But to whom are souls visible? We are somehow left with the awful suspicion that our narrator may have a more accurate insight into the matter.

Introducing his account of Pulheria Ivanovna's death, the narrator remarks that it will seem especially striking because it developed from a very unimportant event. "But according to the strange arrangement of things, trifling causes have always produced great events, and conversely—great undertakings have ended in trifling consequences" (28). As the reader then progresses and learns of the gray cat incident, he is apt to decide that this reversallike pronouncement has been justified: the "trifling" cause of a gray cat's return led to the "great" event of Pulheria Ivanovna's death. But we may also conclude that her "trifling" comment ("A cat is a quiet creature: it won't do evil to anyone") had somehow led to the "great" event of her literally fatal conviction regarding the cat's return. We may even conclude that her strange fear of Afanasy Ivanovich's "teasings" suggests a near realization of normally unsuspected causes. Whatever we conclude, we are left with a disturbing suspicion that our narrator (whoever he is) knows more than he has revealed concerning "the strange arrangement of things."

Notes

1. Similarly, the servants who steal are termed "worthy," and Afanasy Ivanovich, who suspects nothing, "vigilant" (20, 21).

2. Yurij Tynyanov has observed that the opening parallel between dilapidated buildings and dilapidated people is developed throughout the entire story. *Dostoevskij i Gogol'* (Petrograd, 1921), p. 10.

Tynyanov also notes, in connection with what he terms Gogol's "verbal masks," that the pair of old world landowners has the same patronymic (p. 12).

3. This final description contains some typical puns and reversals. "Some sort of *distant* relative arrived from no one knew where." He was "a *terrible* reformer." His "reforms" hasten and complete the deterioration. And: "so *well* did he manage, that within six months the estate was given over to a board of trustees" (38; my emphasis).

"TARAS BULBA"

As Setchkarev has observed, "Taras Bulba" is the least characteristic of Gogol's works.[1] Yet in some respects, it belongs near the center of Gogol's world generally and of *Mirgorod* in particular.[2]

Bulba trains his two sons to be good cossack warriors. Andri, the younger one, falls in love with a Polish girl, fights against the cossacks, and is killed by his own father. Ostap, the elder, is tortured to death by the Poles. Ruthlessly avenging this, Bulba is chained to a tree and burned to death.

As one might expect, Gogol slyly prefigures the love affair and all three deaths. "Taras Bulba," moreover, combines several other Gogolian themes and techniques.

The story opens with a focus on clothes. Bulba derides the clerical robes of his two sons, who have just returned from a religious academy. They regard him sullenly, "like recently released seminarists." "And just one of you try to run!" says Bulba. "I'll watch him fall smack on the ground, all tangled up in his skirts."

Offended, Ostap fights his father, who compliments him. "And you," says Bulba to Andri, "why don't you, son of a dog, give me a pounding?" Here, the boys' mother chides Bulba for forcing his younger son to fight. Bulba calls Andri "a milksop," adding: "Don't listen, son, to your mother: she's a woman, and she knows nothing. What do you want with pampering? Pampering for you—is the open field and a good horse: there's your pampering!"

Much of this anticipates Andri's love affair with the Polish girl and his death by his father's hand in Chapter Nine. Riding out from Polish gates into the open plain (which was termed "pampering"), Andri fights against the cossacks and is suddenly confronted by his father. "Thus a schoolboy, having imprudently poked a classmate and received a blow with a ruler on the forehead in return, flares up like fire . . . and suddenly runs into the teacher, who is entering the room . . ." (II:143). This apparently inappropriate comparison recalls the initial description of the boys ("like seminarists") just before Bulba tried to force Andri to fight him. Here, the "schoolboy" theme is continued as Bulba orders Andri to dismount: "Obediently, like a child, he got off his horse and stopped neither alive nor dead before Taras." Bulba now kills Andri, which tinges the phrase "neither alive nor dead" with eerie truth. He then watches his son fall upon the ground, as he himself had described while joking about the clerical robes. Even Bulba's comment that Andri has died in shame "like a vile dog" seems ironically to echo his earlier taunting of Andri ("son of a dog") to fight him. Moreover, Andri has just been likened, riding out to his death, to a "most handsome, fastest, and youngest borzoi dog" in the "pack" of Polish horsemen (142). As Proffer has observed, high-style and derogatory words for "dog" (*pes* and *sobaka*) are used, respectively, for Andri's glorious appearance and his inglorious death.[3] With further consistency, "son of a dog" had employed the derogatory *sobaka.*

In view of the fact that a woman servant leads Andri to the Polish girl for whom he dies, Bulba's earlier words ("Don't listen, son, to your mother: she's a woman, she knows nothing") can later apply to both women and become almost doubly ironic. The prefiguring is still clearer, however, when the woman servant starts to lead Andri away from the cossack camp at night. Mistaking the situation, Bulba calls out to his son in the darkness: "There's a woman with you! . . . Women will not lead you to good!" (93).

Not all the foreshadowings are so obvious. In Chapter Two, Andri is described as more apt than Ostap to be "the leader of a rather dangerous undertaking" (55). Eventually, this even seems to be an understatement. We also learn that while "listening to philosophical discussions" Andri would see the girl of his dreams before him. This imaginary beauty is described in some detail, which includes a Gogolian focus upon lifelike clothing: "her very dress, which clung about her virginal yet strong limbs, breathed in his dreams with some kind of inexpressible voluptuousness" (56). Much later, as he rides out to his death, we read: "But Andri did not discern who was before him, his own people or some others; he saw nothing. Curls, curls he saw; long, long curls, and a breast like the river swan's, and a snow-white neck, and shoulders, and all that is made for mad kisses" (142-43). Once again his vision of a dream girl, now the Polish one, overpowers and usurps reality. Since Andri is now fighting on the Polish side, the notions "his own people" and "some others" are both Gogolian reversals. Note also the reversallike irony of "nothing," a word followed by an apparent contradiction that proves it to be true.

When Andri first sees the Polish girl, she is framed by a window: "dark-eyed and white, like snow that is illuminated by the morning redness of the sun" (56).[4] A beautiful girl whose white skin is tinged by the sun's glowing light often augurs ill in Gogol's world. When Andri is later led to the Polish girl, the "snow-white semicircles" of her eyes are noted together with the "faint redness" that tinges her face. Near the end, this girl is matter-of-factly presumed to have "bewitched poor Andri" (171). Earlier, Bulba planned revenge upon the girl "who had bewitched" his son: "Her wondrous breasts and shoulders, shining like the never-melting snows that cover mountain peaks, would be crushed against the ground, bloody and covered with dust" (122). In Bulba's dream of revenge, the bewitching glow (on white skin) is replaced by blood (on white snow).

Also typically, Gogol suggestively likens sexual desire in "Taras Bulba" with the appetite for food. Yankel, who reports to Bulba that Andri has joined the other side, describes the Polish girl: "Here the Jew tried, as best he could, to express beauty in his face, extending his arms, squinting one eye and twisting his mouth to the side, as if tasting of something" (112).

When Ostap is tortured to death by the Poles, Bulba (disguised) watches helplessly in the enormous crowd of Polish spectators. (This is a slight twist of the Gogolian theme of an unseen audience.) Just before he dies, the brave Ostap weakens and cries: "Father, where are you? Do you hear?" (165). The words "I hear!" ring out loudly, causing the entire crowd to shudder. Bulba then escapes, as Gogol employs his "already" device [5] : Yankel looks around to see Bulba, "but Taras already was not near him: not a trace of him remained."

Introducing the tortures, Gogol also gives the technique of "de-familiarization" (or "making strange" [6]) an unusual twist. A Polish gentleman describes the scene to his sweetheart in a silk dress. "All these people, sweetie," he explains, "have come to see the criminals executed . . . and when they cut off his head, sweetie, he'll die at once . . . he, sweetie, will no longer have a head" (162-63). Though perhaps overdone, the insertion of "sweetie" produces an ironic contrast that intensifies the defamiliarization.

Ostap's tortures are not described, but we are told that he remained bravely silent even while the bones of his arms and legs began to break with a terrible cracking sound (164). Early in

Chapter Two, this was perhaps prefigured by the "awful floggings" that Ostap stoically endured at the academy (53). Even before this, when Bulba welcomes Ostap home in Chapter One, he rather jokingly guesses that the lad was often beaten. "There's no use remembering the past," Ostap answers "indifferently." "What was—is over with!" (45).

While introducing Taras Bulba to the reader, Gogol is already partially focusing upon Bulba's death, which concludes the story. Bulba, we are informed, was a person who could only have existed in the battle-scarred South of fifteenth-century Russia, which had been "burnt to ashes by the savage onslaughts of predatory Mongolians . . . when man . . . settled on the ashes . . . when the age-old pacific Slav spirit was enveloped by martial flames . . ." (46). More than a hundred pages later, Bulba is captured by the Poles, chained to a tree, and burned to death by a bonfire (170). He is thus literally "enveloped by martial flames" and "burnt to ashes," and his story shifts from ashes ("settled on the ashes") to man to ashes again. This same introductory paragraph also mentioned "the flint of misfortunes" and "words" like "sparks, which had fallen on dry wood."

The most subtle prefiguring, however, occurs near the very end. Bulba (who, to avenge Ostap, is burning Polish girls "together with the altars" where they had sought sanctuary and hurling infants "into the flames") is captured by the Poles because he hesitates in battle in order to recover his lost pipe. "Stop!" he shouts. "I don't want the enemy Poles to get even my pipe!" (170). Within half a paragraph, Taras is being burned to death. (Curiously enough, a pipe also portends death in "The Terrible Vengeance" and "Viy" but there, the suggestions turn on *double entendre* rather than the idea of burning.)

Finally, among the horrors described in "Taras Bulba," we may note a Gogolian eerie point of view. When the cossack warrior Borodaty is killed: "A stern cossack soul rose up to the high heavens, frowning and indignant, yet also marveling that it had flown out so early from such a mighty body" (119). While the description at first seems typical of folklore deaths in battle, a Gogolian twist raises the question of how our narrator could have such insight into the "feelings" of a soul. A similar eeriness enhances the foreshadowing of disaster. When Bulba falls asleep, musing about how to avenge himself upon the Polish girl who had "bewitched" Andri, we read: "But Bulba did not know what God was preparing for man on the morrow . . ." (122). The morrow, of course, brings Bulba's apparently free act of killing his son Andri.

Notes

1. Setchakarev, p. 143.

2. Edmund Wilson seems right (though the reasons he gives are rather incomplete) that "Taras Bulba" is closer to Gogol's later work than various critics have been "willing to admit." *A Window on Russia* (New York, 1972), p. 43.

3. Proffer, p. 172.

4. After she has left Kiev, Andri sees in her place "some kind of fat face looking out of the window" (58).

5. See discussion here of "The Terrible Vengeance."

6. Discussed here in "Christmas Eve."

"VIY"

Three seminarists spend the night at a farm. One of them, Homa, encounters a witch who rides on his back in an eerie moonlit scene. He then rides on her back; she collapses and changes into a beautiful girl.

Miles away, a beautiful girl returns home from a walk exhausted and fatally injured. Her dying wish is that the philosophy student Homa should read the last rites and prayers over her body for three nights. He is forced to do so, and on the third night in church, her corpse calls in Viy, the terrible chief of the gnomes whose eyelids reach to the very ground. Homa dies of fright. His two former comrades later agree that all the women who sit at the market in Kiev are witches.

As the story begins, we see the seminarists leaving Kiev for the summer: theologian Halyava, philosopher Homa, and rhetorician Gorobets. As night falls, they become lost. Homa tries shouting. His voice fades away in the dark, seeming to elicit no reply. "Soon after, however, they heard a weak moaning that resembled a wolf's howl" (II:182). Halyava proposes sleeping in the open field, but Homa, we read, "could not agree to that." He was hungry. "Moreover, despite his jolly disposition, the philosopher was somewhat afraid of wolves."

The seminarists push on. They are overjoyed when they "seemed to hear barking." After this, an old woman lets them sleep at her farm, where Homa's ultimately fatal adventure begins. Later, when he walks to the church for his third reading, we are told that

> The night was hellish. A whole pack of wolves was howling in the distance. Even the very barking of the dogs was somehow terrifying.
> "It seems as if something else is howling: that's not wolves," said Dorosh. (215-16) [1]

What seemed to be barking, we may recall, had helped the seminarists to find the fateful farm. Finally, when the corpse cries "Bring in Viy! Go get Viy!" the ensuing silence is broken by "the howling of wolves in the distance, and soon the sound of heavy footsteps reached the church" (217). Viy then appears, and the circle is complete. Seeking to avoid wolves, Homa is led by what seems to be barking to an adventure which eventually results in his death from a supernatural encounter which is both anticipated, and attended, by what seems to be barking and the howling of wolves.

As in "Christmas Eve" and "The Enchanted Place," references to the devil in "Viy" gradually seem to acquire ironic accuracy. When night falls and the seminarists become lost, Homa exclaims: "What the devil!" (182). "My God," he soon adds, "you can't even see the devil's fist." He thus literally surrounds "God" with two (eventually quite appropriate) mentions of the devil. Homa also offers to pay the old woman in return for some food, softly adding: "Damned [literally, "About two devils"] if you'll get anything!" (184). She answers that they should be satisfied with a place to sleep: "What fastidious young gentlemen the devil has brought!"

When Homa first appears in the story, we learn that he is very fond of smoking his pipe (*lyul'ku;* 181). This is the same word (meaning "pipe" or "cradle") that prefigures the death of Danilo's son in "The Terrible Vengeance" and here in *Mirgorod,* the death of Taras Bulba. After his nocturnal adventure with the witch, Homa stretches out in a tavern, "smoking, as was his custom, his pipe (*lyul'ku*)" (188). He, we read, was "already not thinking at all about his unusual [2] experience." Later, we hear a rumor that the witch once murdered a tiny child in its cradle (*lyul'ke*). The mother had heard a dog howling ominously, and when she opened the door, the dog, who was now the girl/witch, ran up to the cradle and bit the child's throat (204). Thus, Gogol subtle interweaves two sinister themes: the howling of dogs/wolves and the death-portending pipe/cradle. Even before this, we read of servants who liked to smoke a pipe (*lyul'ku*) and to speak of everyday things including "who had seen a wolf" (200-01).

"Viy" repeatedly displays a Gogolian association of the human appetites for food and for sex. When the witch appears to Homa, she approaches him with outstretched arms. "Listen," he says, "it is Lent now; and I'm a person who even for a thousand gold pieces wouldn't break a fast" (185). After his adventure, however, Homa winks at a young widow, whereupon he "was the very same day fed

with wheat dumplings, chicken . . . and, in a word, it is impossible to
enumerate what he had at the table, laid in a little clay hut in the
middle of a cherry orchard" (188). Note that while the camera
moves away from this little scene, catching even the house and the
land around it, focus still seems to be closing in upon the lovers.

Trying to avoid reading over the girl's corpse, Homa vigorously
denies his devoutness, adding that he recently "paid the baker's wife
a visit, Holy Thursday notwithstanding" (197). Doughy foods are
sometimes associated with a woman's body in Gogol's works, and
both the "wheat dumplings" (in the passage quoted above) and the
idea of a "baker's wife" possibly reflect this general theme.

These suggestions of "sexual appetite" are amplified by two Gogolian references to clothing as revealing what it contains and obscures. Having fortified himself with liquor for the ordeal of reading
over the corpse, Homa, we learn, was hit on the back with a spade by
a young woman "when he took it into his head to grope and inves-
tigate what sort of material her blouse and skirt were made of"
(209). There is also a "frightful flirt" in the story who wears a
"tightly fitting dress, which displayed her round and powerful
figure" (211).

Preceded by what Homa (apparently) mistakes for a sexual invitation, the two nocturnal rides (the witch on his back, then reversed)
seem strangely suggestive. Indeed, Leon Stilman has aptly applied
the term "witch-bride-to-be."[3] For Homa twice feels that his experience, though exhausting and unpleasant, is oddly "sweet"
(186,187). Moreover, as Stilman also notes, Homa sees "fantastic
and even seductive scenes" while the witch rides on his back. This
suggestiveness is further developed by a rumor that the witch (as the
beautiful young girl) showed her "naked, full, and white little foot"
to a peasant who then let her ride him like a horse and afterward
burned to death "all by himself" (203). Still later, the peasants play
a game wherein people ride on each other's backs. "Homa unsuccessfully tried to enter into this game: some sort of dark thought, like
a nail, was stuck in his head" (209). Homa is of course preoccupied
about his impending task of reading over the corpse. But note the
reversal word "unsuccessfully," which reveals that the back-riding
game, in which he hopes to forget the witch, makes him remember
her.

Homa was led to the sheep's pen by a person repeatedly termed "old woman" *(starukha;* 183-85). Just after this, the witch appears and is termed *starukha* five times in only a few lines (185). The reader is thus induced to presume that Homa's hostess is also the witch. And since the witch is really a beautiful young girl, the false focus may well be double.

Gogol employs his technique of broken description (which often attends a possible overlapping of two realities) three times in "Viy": when Homa decides the old woman is a witch, when he notices that his surroundings are mysteriously transformed, and when the witch changes back to her beautiful girl aspect. The broken descriptions are, respectively: "a black, like coal, forest" (186): "transparent, like a mountain stream, water" (186); "with long, like arrows, eyelashes" (188). We may also observe that the witch/beautiful-girl's body seems to exist in, or span, two realities (rather like the witch's/cat's hand/paw and Levko's note in "May Night . . ."; a roll of coins in "The Portrait"; and of course "The Enchanted Place" itself).

Gogolian reversals tend to question the surface of reality in the nocturnal scene. Instead of being on land, Homa suddenly seems to be carrying the witch above water; instead of a moon, a strange sun seems to be shining. After the witch rides on Homa's back he (reversely) rides on hers. At this point, the grass again seems to be on land and the moon "replaces" the sun, reversing the reversal and leaving the reader with an uneasy doubt as to which reality was more real. Finally, when Homa sees the corpse of the beautiful girl, a part of the preceding reversal is echoed: the girl's "brows—were like night amid a sunny day" (199).

Gogol makes intricate use of interlocking detail while describing the rhetorician Gorobets.

> He wore only a long forelock, and hence his character at that time was still little developed; but judging from the large bumps on his forehead, with which he often appeared in class, one could suppose that he would become a good warrior. Theologian Halyava and philosopher Homa often pulled him by the forelock as a sign of their protectorship and used him in the capacity of errand boy. (181)

Throughout this passage, focus frequently centers on Gorobets' head. At first, the notion that his long forelock signifies undeveloped character seems merely a mocking of cause and effect. When we learn that his older companions often pulled his forelock, however, it appears that the boy's "character" may really be "developing" from the hair-pullings. In this sense, the pulled hair and growing bumps amusingly combine to suggest constant development upon the "head" of the young "rhetorician." This odd consistency of association resembles that in the head and garden rake episode (Preface One to *Evenings*); in the treatment of grandfather's head ("The Lost Letter"); in what befalls Havronya's hat ("The Sorochintsy Fair"); and in a humorous digression in "Rome." [4]

Early in "Viy," we are told that the seminarists sometimes put on a play "in which case some theologian, whose height was only a little lower than the Kiev belfry, would distinguish himself by representing Herodias or Pentefria, spouse of the Egyptian courtier" (179). This casual and somewhat comic (note the reversal word "lower") generalization seems to have little to do with the story as a whole. Yet "Viy" opens with a ringing of the monastery bell in Kiev, and at the end, we learn that Halyava has been made bell ringer of the highest Kiev belfry. In addition, Herodias and Pentefria (Potiphar's wife) are women who inflicted punishments upon men (Herodias had John the Baptist beheaded; Potiphar's wife had Joseph cast in prison for resisting her advances). In "Viy," the witch ultimately has Homa killed for resisting her advances. (She approaches him, we recall, with outstretched arms.) Very casually then, this little "digression" may be seen to anticipate some of the plot that follows. The effect resembles that of the mayor's (ignored) prophetic dream early in *The Government Inspector*.

Notes

1. In the Russian, sound abets the effect *(Volki vyli vdali)*.

2. "Unusual" is *neobyknovennom*.

3. Leon Stilman, "Men, Women, and Matchmakers," in *Gogol from the Twentieth Century*, Robert A. Maguire, trans. and ed. (Princeton, N.J., 1974), p. 397.

4. The Italian Peppe, who, like Shponka, constantly consults a fortune-telling book, is about to fight another man when the latter calls him a "calf's head" (III:233). Peppe strikes himself "on the forehead," rushes off, and buys a lottery ticket whose number is the same as that of "calf's head" in his fortune-telling book.

"THE TALE OF HOW IVAN IVANOVICH
QUARRELED WITH IVAN NIKIFOROVICH"

As in "Christmas Eve," where he participates more overtly as well, the devil lurks behind and shapes the surface of this story. The surface? I.I. is called a "gander" by I.N., whose gun he wishes to obtain in trade. Years later, the friends are almost reconciled when the insult is vividly recalled, freezing the quarrel in apparently endless legal proceedings.

The two Ivans, we learn at the outset, "are between themselves such friends as the world has not produced. Anton Prokofevich Pupopuz, who even now still goes about in a brown frock coat with light blue sleeves and dines on Sundays at the judge's, often used to say that the devil himself had tied Ivan Nikiforovich and Ivan Ivanovich together with a string" (II:225-26). Here, a digression which seems to obscure the Ivans actually leads to the judge, who will figure so prominently in their lives. Moreover, the Ivans are said to be joined by the devil. Gogol's reverse vision stresses the friends' closeness even while taking the first step toward undermining it. Note also the literal meaning of "such friends as the world has not produced."

The two friends' comic symmetry suggests a fitting together: "Ivan Ivanovich's head resembles a radish, tail downward; the head of Ivan Nikiforovich, a radish, tail upward." (226) Rumor suggests that "Ivan Nikiforovich was born with a tail behind him" (226). This notion is then humorously refuted since (1) only witches, and only a few of them, have tails, and (2) witches are more often female than male. But this hardly reassures us. As a result of Gogolian reverse vision, praise is often undermined. In fact, the two Ivans are soon labeled "rare friends" with an adjective *(redkie)* which also signifies "seldom"—a prophetic play of meaning indeed.

When Ivan Ivanovich arrives to bargain for the gun, his friend mentions the devil in speaking about the hot weather. "You just would mention the devil," Ivan Ivanovich replies. "Mark my words, or it'll be too late: you'll catch it in the next world [*na tom svete*] for such ungodly language" (232). And when Ivan Ivanovich offers his brown pig for the gun, his friend rementions the devil. "Again! You

4. Drawings by P. Boklevsky (1882)

just can't get along without the devil. It's a sin . . . !" (235). This is countered by a Gogolian remark that the devil knows what a pig is. Next, Ivan Ivanovich adds two sacks of oats to his offer.

> "Two sacks for the gun?"
> "Not two empty sacks, but full of oats; and have you forgotten the pig?"
> "You can go and kiss your pig, and if you don't want to, then go kiss the devil." (236)

At this point, Ivan Ivanovich is again moved to predict disaster for his friend "in the next world" *(na tom svete)* for such ungodly language. A few lines later, Ivan Nikiforovich utters the fatal appellation, "gander." And the devil-associated pig which Ivan Nikiforovich apparently "forgets" is the same one that later steals his petition against Ivan Ivanovich. (It has not yet been copied, and this further ensnarls the legal aspects of the altercation.) Still later, when I.N. learns that I.I.'s pig has stolen his petition, he asks: "Wasn't it the brown one?" (261). The mayor has just threatened to lock up and sentence the brown sow like a person (260)—a ridiculous animal-human reversal that seems strangely justified. And to complete the irony, Ivan Ivanovich twice calls the devil-associated pig "God's creature!" (259,260).

At last, when the Ivans are on the point of being reconciled, Ivan Nikiforovich declares:

> "Let me tell you as a friend, Ivan Ivanovich! . . . you took offense at the devil knows what: at my calling you a gander. . . ."
> Ivan Nikiforovich immediately realized his blunder in pronouncing this word; but it was too late: the word has been pronounced.
> Everything went to the devil! (273)

And there, with the devil, the matter remains, each Ivan confident that the eternal case will soon be settled in his favor. "It is boring in this world [*na ètom svete*], ladies and gentlemen!" is Gogol's ending, which can be read with the emphasis: "It is boring in *this* world, ladies and gentlemen!" For the phrase "in this world" is but one letter removed from the phrase repeatedly used to suggest punishment by the devil: "in the next world" *(na tom svete)*. And this seems a further suggestion that the Ivans were indeed "such friends as the world [*svet*] has not produced." When the rift between the Ivans first becomes established, we read: "What worthy people! Is there anything solid in this world?" *(na ètom svete)*.

Arriving to bargain for the coveted gun, Ivan Ivanovich seems almost to step for a moment into some other dimension.

> The room into which Ivan Ivanovich entered was completely dark, because the shutters were closed, and a ray of sunlight, passing through a hole made in the shutter, acquired a rainbow-like color and, striking the opposite wall, sketched on it a multicolored landscape of thatched roofs, trees and clothes hanging in the yard, except that everything had a transformed aspect. This imparted to the whole room some kind of uncanny twilight.
> "God help us!" said Ivan Ivanovich. (231–32)

After an innocent beginning, this passage abruptly swerves past contradiction (the room was not "completely dark") toward impossibility (a ray of light "sketches"?) only to wobble off precariously along the edge of eerie reconciliation (the "sketch" was however transformed, and thus its "aspect" was somewhat unrecognizable). But how, one wonders, can a ray of light sketch? And what narrator could detect such a "sketch" in its transformed aspect? (At the end of "Nevsky Prospect," the narrator presumes that Satan lights the street lamps "just to show everything in an unreal aspect.")

And why, in the present tale, does Ivan Ivanovich, upon entering this eerie room, exclaim: "God save us!"? Is he merely unaccustomed to the "uncanny twilight"? It seems possible that Gogol had in mind a sort of "optical memory" that he describes elsewhere [1] (Ivan Ivanovich has just come in from seeing the "original" landscape, bathed in bright sunlight). Yet this room now becomes the stage upon which The Quarrel is born. And since the devil seems to direct much of what happens, the "uncanny twilight" seems an appropriate setting.

Even excluding the devil, the "Ivans" tale is most Gogolian. Clothes, not people, receive the initial focus. As the story opens, we are urged "for God's sake" to feast our eyes upon Ivan Ivanovich's astrakhan (fur) coat from the side, "especially if he starts talking with someone." Ivan Ivanovich is thus introduced while speaking. The paragraph then trails off into apparent absurdity: Ivan's magnificent coat was made even before Agafiya Fedoseevna traveled to Kiev. "Do you know Agafiya Fedoseevna? The very same one who bit off the ear of the assessor." Somehow developing out of the image of Ivan Ivanovich conversing, this sudden idea of ear-biting strangely anticipates the "painful" word he will later hear in conversation with the other Ivan. And the person who later visits Ivan Nikiforovich—and who continually keeps the quarrel going—is also called Agafiya Fedoseevna, though she is then introduced as if for the first time. (Note also the playful question to the reader: "Do you know Agafiya Fedoseevna?")

Our initial picture of Ivan Ivanovich conversing also leads to his

gift of speaking exceedingly pleasantly. Lord, how he speaks! It can only be compared with the sensation you have when someone searches your head, or ever so gently draws a finger across your heel. You listen, listen, and lower your head. So pleasant! Exceedingly pleasant! Like sleep after a good bath. (226)

Whatever "pleasantness" one detects here seems tainted by vaguely uncomfortable sensations. Elusive fleas (or worse),[2] evoked by "searching," suggest a hidden irritation behind whatever pleasure one feels. The stroked heel further develops this uncomfortable tickling sensation, while the naked foot leads to the bath with Gogolian precarious logic: the bath may be seen as a measure to remove the fleas. Similarly, the lowered head seems strangely compatible with the post-bath nap. And though the nap may indeed be purely pleasant, it seems oddly benumbing as a reaction to Ivan Ivanovich's eloquence. Later, of course, this same pleasant elo-

quence (reversely) prods Ivan Nikiforovich into pronouncing the
fatal word "gander."

Early in the story, we read: "Ivan Ivanovich has a somewhat
timorous nature. Ivan Nikiforovich, on the other hand, wears
trousers with such wide folds that if they were blown out you could
put the whole yard, barns, and buildings into them" (227). At first
glance, this seems like a rather silly non sequitur. Yet in contrast to a
"timorous nature," the "blown-out trousers" may be seen to swell up
quite aggressively, much as a cat, hissing, puffs up and arches its
back. We may also note the Gogolian theme of "live" clothes. Ivan
Ivanovich soon watches an old woman taking things out to air in the
yard. "What a stupid woman!" he thinks. "Now she'll probably
drag out Ivan Nikiforovich himself for an airing!" (229). Then we
are told that "Ivan Ivanovich was not entirely mistaken in his
conjecture. After about five minutes, Ivan Nikiforovich's nankeen
trousers rose up and occupied almost half the yard. After that she
also carried out his cap and his gun." The aggressively blown-out
trousers now aptly prefigure the Ivan who will pronounce the
"gander" insult. And the appropriate item over which they will
quarrel—his gun—also appears.

Ivan Ivanovich's desire for this gun is presented as an ironic
reversal. Gazing upon his property early in Chapter Two, he smugly
wonders: "What don't I have?" And, after an enumeration of his
riches: "what else don't I have? . . . I'd like to know what I don't
have." After this, of course, he sees the gun and covets it intensely.
Gogol, we may note, favors ironically prophetic negation: Ivan
wonders three times what he doesn't have. (The wording resembles
the opening of "Nevsky Prospect": "What this street does not shine
with . . . !") And here, a similar effect seems to work in reverse. Just
after Ivan Ivanovich vengefully chops down the (humorously appropriate) goose pen of Ivan Nikiforovich, the next chapter begins:
"Mirgorod is a wonderful town! What buildings it doesn't have!"
(224).

As Setchkarev has noted, Ivan Ivanovich has "a swarm of ille-
gitimate children," amusingly presented through "the description of
his maid Gapka and *her* children." [3] The humor derives partly from
juxtaposition: "He had no children. Gapka does have children, who

often run about the yard" (224). We then learn that Ivan is suspiciously partial to Gapka's children, and that Gapka is "a healthy wench . . . with fresh calves and cheeks." Later, I.N. refers to I.I.'s children, and one of them calls I.I. "Daddy" (240). More subtly, "Gapka's" numerous children may be seen to reinforce quite remarkably the Chief Priest's conviction that "no one . . . knew how to live like Ivan Ivanovich" (224).

And what of the other bachelor, Ivan Nikiforovich? Agafiya Fedoseevna visits him "for whole weeks and sometimes even more" (240). She, "it would seem," had "absolutely no reason" to visit him. Upon arriving, however, she "would take the entire house in her hands."

> I must confess I do not understand why it is so arranged, that women should seize us by the nose just as deftly as they do the handle of a teapot? Either their hands are so created, or our noses are not good for anything else. And no matter that Ivan Nikiforovich's nose looked rather like a plum, still she seized him by that nose and led him after her like a little dog. When she was there he even changed, involuntarily, his usual way of life: he did not lie in the sun so long, and if he did lie, it was not in the nude, but he always put on a shirt and wide trousers, although Agafiya Fedoseevna absolutely did not demand this. She was not one to stand on ceremony, and, when Ivan Nikiforovich had a fever, she herself with her own hands rubbed him down from head to foot with turpentine and vinegar. . . . Her whole figure resembled a large tub, and for this reason it was just as hard to find her waist as to see one's own nose without a mirror. Her legs were nice and short, formed in the shape of two pillows. (241)

As developed here, the phrase "taking the entire house in her hands" refers in large measure to the nose and naked body of Ivan Nikiforovich. Whatever the relationship between these two blimplike people, Ivan's "nose" does seem a playful euphemism. It is likened to a "plum," and Gogol often associates the appetites for food and sex. And though the "plum" presumably does not stick out very far from Ivan's obese body, Agafiya seems to have little trouble in "seizing" it. Here, Gogol's image of a roundish teapot with its little lower spout (often called a "little nose [*nosik*]" in Russian) becomes ingenious indeed. Part of the humor derives from ironically suggestive negation: "our noses are not good for anything else . . . he did not lie . . . it was not in the nude." This seems especially so since Ivan must be pictured in the (just denied) nude, as well as in a (just denied) prone position for his rubdowns. Even the third denial humorously deteriorates (through sexual analogy): "our noses are not good for anything else."

As often happens with Gogol, the title of the "Ivans" tale expands in meaning as the reader progresses. At first, one has the impression that the story will focus upon a quarrel. Actually, there are perhaps two quarrels. Or perhaps there are no quarrels (each "quarrel" consists of the single word "gander" and very little else except protracted silence). Gogol does however interweave several (mostly devil-related elements: the devil's protean involvement in the prelude to the "quarrel"; playful but ominous hints at "the next world"; an "uncanny twilight" setting for the "quarrel" itself; an undercurrent of furtive sex (a further Gogolian hint of the devil's presence?); and numerous forward-leaning and interlocking details, including a devil-associated pig (which figures both in fomenting and in prolonging the hostilities). Given the devil's invisible, but presumably quite active role in the story, one can, perhaps, finally view it as a tale of *how* Ivan Ivanovich quarreled with Ivan Nikiforovich.

Notes

1. In "The Hetman," Gogol declares: "There is no complete darkness for the eye. It always, no matter how one clenches it, sketches and presents the colors it has seen" (III:306). The ensuing narration describes a fantasy of shapes and designs not unlike Nabokov's praedormitary visions in *Speak, Memory*.

2. Two pages later, we are told that both Ivans greatly disliked fleas.

3. Setchkarev, p. 149.

CHAPTER 4

Tales

"NEVSKY PROSPECT"

Strolling along Nevsky Prospect, the artist Piskaryov and Lieutenant Pirogov separate—each to follow a beautiful girl. The unsuccessful results of their quests comprise the two halves of this
intricately symmetrical story, which Pushkin (in 1836) called "the
fullest" of Gogol's works.[1]

As "Nevsky Prospect" begins, we are told: "What this street does
not shine with—the beautiful girl [*krasavitsa*] of our capital!" (III:9).
The story ends with a description of Nevsky at night, "when the
entire town turns into thunder and gleaming light" and Satan lights
the street lamps "just to show everything in an unreal aspect." The
opening exclamation becomes ironically prophetic.

Early in the story, we learn that "Nevsky Prospect is still more
pleasing to ladies." At the end, one is advised "not to trust this
Nevsky Prospect!" and to "trust ladies least of all." The initial
comparison of the street to a beautiful girl proves almost disturbingly appropriate. Also consistently, the two young ladies who are
unsuccessfully followed are each considered "a beautiful girl" (*krasavitsa*, 18,22; 40).[2]

5. Sketch by Nikolai Gogol

An early description of Nevsky shows the ladies with their fluttery handkerchiefs:

It seems as if an entire sea of butterflies has suddenly risen up from flower stalks in an agitated, shining cloud above the black beetles of the male sex. Here, you will meet such waists as you have never even dreamed of: thin, slender little waists not at all thicker than the neck of a bottle, which, when meeting them you respectfully step to one side so as not to nudge them carelessly with an impolite elbow; your heart is possessed by timidness and fear, lest even your careless breath should cause to snap in two the most charming production of nature and art. And what ladies' sleeves you will meet on Nevsky Prospect! Oh, how charming! They somewhat resemble two aerial balloons, so that a lady might suddenly rise up into the air if she were not supported by a man; for it is just as easy and pleasant to lift a lady into the air as to raise a glass brimming with champagne to one's mouth. (12-13)

This passage appropriately focuses upon the women one may meet on Nevsky Prospect, plus some dangers that may be involved. It also builds up an image of two halves joined vulnerably together. First, we see butterfly-like handkerchiefs, then small-waisted dresses, also delicate and buoyant. This compound image then reappears as the champagne glass, also seen as rising in the air. Finally, the glass is pictured approaching one's mouth, from which a "breath" might "snap" the stemlike waists of the ladies. Gogolian focus thus typically lingers while apparently moving away.

Perhaps yet more remarkably, the hourglasslike image developed by this passage seems to reflect and reinforce the symmetrical structuring of the entire story. And it does so while treating in miniature the central themes: men meeting beautiful women who are apt to be snapped in two, especially if "nudged" or "raised," plus an ecstatically "shining" surface that "seems" glorious ("It seems . . . shining cloud") but proves quite dangerous ("your heart is possessed by timidness and fear"). Even the danger, associated here with "bottle" and "champagne glass," seems faintly in keeping with the two heroes' misfortunes: the opium drunk by Piskaryov and the return of a tipsy Schiller and his drunken comrades to surprise and pummel Pirogov.

Gogol's introductory description of a typical day on Nevsky aptly ends with a lighting of the street lamps: "It is then that a mysterious time arrives, when the lamps give everything a kind of enticing, wondrous light. . . . At that time one senses some sort of goal, or, better, something that resembles a goal, something exceedingly unaccountable . . ." (15). Here, the reversal word "better" (in conjunction with "resembles a goal") anticipates the futile nature of both pursuits.

Soon after this, as Piskaryov follows the girl of his choice, we read: "the beautiful girl looked back, and it seemed to him as if a faint smile flashed upon her lips. He shook all over and did not trust his eyes. No, the lamp with its deceptive light had conveyed to her face the likeness of a smile . . ." (18). Here, "beautiful girl" is *krasavitsa,* the word used initially to describe Nevsky Prospect. "Trust" *(veril)* is one of Gogol's favorite warning words, and as seen above, the ending tells us to "trust" neither Nevsky nor the women we meet there.

When they first catch sight of the two beauties, Pirogov advises his artist friend to pursue the brunette, since he finds her so attractive. Blushing, Piskaryov retorts: "As if she's one of those women who walk along Nevsky Prospect in the evening. . . !" (15-16). This is of course precisely what she turns out to be. Gogol also has the naïve, hopeful Piskaryov imagine, while following the brunette, "that from him, surely, some meaningful services would be required . . ." (20). When we learn that the girl is a prostitute, the notion of "requiring services" becomes ironically reversed. Piskaryov soon follows the girl up a winding staircase, and she says: "Walk more carefully!"—an unwittingly accurate warning indeed.

Eventually, the fatally disillusioned Piskaryov tries to escape by means of opium, and: "dreams became his life" (25). This reversal is intensified by his desperate dreams of the brunette, wherein she repeatedly asks how he ever could have imagined her to be a prostitute (26,29). Finally, Piskaryov visits the girl in real life and proposes marriage, saying that they both could work to overcome his poverty. Her reply is a darkly humorous reversal: Surely he does not expect her to "take up working" (32).

After this, Piskaryov cuts his throat, and we return to Lieutenant Pirogov, last seen following the blonde and thinking, with a smug smile, "that there was no beauty able to resist him" (16). Still in close pursuit, he now thinks: "You, darling, are mine!" (34). Here, Gogol interrupts Pirogov to describe the society to which he belonged. The ensuing digression (which twice employs the reversal word "better") tells us amusingly little about Pirogov, though it does describe a type of pale, frivolous "beautiful girl" who is easily impressed by men of his stamp but who often rewards them with words only. This rambling digression anticipates much of what follows. Even while reading it, one may picture Pirogov, still smugly following his "frivolous" blonde and already beginning to "impress" her.

A crudely humorous false focus introduces the blonde's husband, whose name is "Schiller, not the Schiller who wrote *Wilhelm Tell* and *The History of the Thirty Years' War*, but the well-known Schiller, the accomplished tinsmith of Meshchanskaya Street" (37).

This foolishness leads to the slapstick scene now witnessed by Pirogov. The drunken Schiller is begging his drunken friend Hoffmann ("not the writer Hoffmann, but the rather good shoemaker of Officer Street") to cut off his, Schiller's, nose. (His hope is to avoid expenditures for snuff.)

> And except for the sudden appearance of Lieutenant Pirogov, Hoffmann, without any doubt, would quite matter-of-factly have cut off Schiller's nose, because he had already placed his knife in such a position as if he wished to cut out a sole for a shoe. (38)

The humorously uncanny point of view here (how can all this be evident from the position of the knife?) is rendered strangely appropriate by a Gogolian haunting return. For the very shape of the sole to be cut out by shoemaker Hoffmann seems oddly similar to the flat area remaining after the amputation of a human nose.

Despite Schiller's attempts to dissuade him, Pirogov sustains contact with the blonde by ordering a pair of new spurs. Giving the order to Schiller's wife, he claims that "in order to love" her, a bridle would be more appropriate than spurs (39). His second order is yet more suggestive. "I have a very fine Turkish dagger," says Pirogov, "but I'd like to have another sheath made to fit it" (41).

Here, Gogol digresses to describe the precise German Schiller.

> His exactness extended to a regulation of not kissing his wife more than twice in twenty-four hours; and in order not to kiss an extra time, he never put more than one teaspoonful of pepper in his soup; on Sunday, however, this rule was not so strictly observed, because then Schiller would drink two bottles of beer and a bottle of caraway brandy, though he always swore at it. (42)

The humorous non sequitur of this passage abruptly forks into two possibilities: does Schiller "kiss" his wife more on Sundays, or less? If the liquor consumed removes Schiller's inhibitions, we may expect "more," yet his final mood seems almost to suggest "less." Whatever, the notion of "kissing on Sunday" receives a Gogolian twist. A few days later, Pirogov passes by Schiller's house, sees his wife in the window, and asks about her husband. "He's not at home on Sundays," says "the foolish little blond" (43). The next Sunday, Pirogov arrives and seems to be dancing quite successfully with the blonde, when Schiller returns home with two friends and beats him up. Thus, both Pirogov's smug expectations and Piskaryov's naïve hopes remain unrealized.

Was Pirogov, then, also deceived by the "evil shine" of Nevsky Prospect? Apparently so. In the famous closing paragraph, we read that "all is not what it seems!"

> Do you imagine that those two fat men who have stopped in front of a church being built are discussing its architecture? Not at all: they are speaking of how strangely two crows are sitting, each facing the other. Do you think that that enthusiast, who is waving his arms, is speaking of how his wife threw a ball from the window to an officer he did not know in the least? Not at all. . . . (45-6)

In this apparently rambling passage, the image of two halves joined together, elaborately developed before, twice reappears. The two fat men and the two crows, both facing each other, form a double image that reflects and reinforces still further the architecture of the entire story. The full sequence of strangely related shapes may now be seen as follows: butterflies, small-waisted dresses, champagne glass, two silhouetted fat men, two silhouetted crows, and the two symmetrical halves of the story itself.

Finally, the wife who throws a ball from the window to an unknown officer oddly recalls the blonde who told Lieutenant Pirogov from the window that her husband was not at home on Sundays. Moreover, the abrupt shattering of this picture ("not at all") seems to parallel the abrupt, shattering appearance of Schiller and his friends at home on Sunday. Thus, the ending of this intricately symmetrical story applies to both Piskaryov and Pirogov, bewitched by the sinister evening light that was always there, from the very beginning, behind the glorious, shining splendor of Nevsky Prospect, "the beautiful girl of our capital."

Notes

1. A. S. Pushkin, *Polnoe sobranie sochinenij v desyati tomakh* (Moscow, 1962-66), VII, 345.

2. Yet another interconnection is the expression "it seems," first used repeatedly to describe the glorious beauty of Nevsky Prospect; then, at the end: "All is deception, all is a dream, all is not what it seems!"

Gogol also wove some additional prophetic irony into his description of a typical day on Nevsky: "What a rapid fantasmagoria passes over it in the course of only one day: How many changes it does not undergo in the course of twenty-four hours!" (10). In the Russian, the word "undergo" *(vyterpit)* can also mean "suffer" or "endure."

"THE NOSE"

Viktor Vinogradov has extensively related this strange story to what he terms the "nosology" that pervaded the literary and non-literary atmosphere of the 1820s and 1830s.[1] He has also related "The Nose" to mentions of noses in many of Gogol's other writings, including a letter in which Gogol confused "a furious desire" to be transformed into a single huge nose, the better to imbibe the fragrances of spring.[2]

In terms of the present study, "The Nose" may be viewed as a reversal of waking and sleeping worlds: both the drunken barber and his apparent victim awake into a nightmarelike reality.[3] (Vinogradov refers to this parallel awakening three times; in its initial form, he notes, the tale was to have been a dream.[4]) Yet another Gogolian reversal in "The Nose" may be identified with the efforts of various critics to turn the human body upside down in search of sexual analogy.[5]

The story opens by referring to "an unusually strange occurrence," a label that seems less and less redundant as one reads further.[6] A barber whose surname is lost even from his sign (which however clearly states: "Also let blood") awakens to recognize, in his breakfast bread, the nose of his customer Kovalyov. The "bloodletting," of course, suggests that the barber was responsible for this (never explained) accident. It also anticipates Kovalyov's darkly humorous attempt to conceal his noselessness by covering his face with a handkerchief "as if his nose were bleeding" (III:54).

Throughout the tale, Gogol (reversely) describes fantastic events in matter-of-fact terms. The barber, we are casually told, recognizes the nose as Kovalyov's (just as the latter does later, when it is person-sized, dressed in uniform, and outranks him). "The devil knows how this was done," observes the barber, and perhaps one must ultimately believe him.

Afraid that he may be caught by a policeman, whom he vividly envisions in silver-embroidered uniform, with a saber, the barber takes the nose out to dispose of it. And as part of a striking parallel with Yuri Olesha's *Envy*,[7] the barber finally drops the nose, wrapped in a rag, from a bridge. At this point a policeman, complete with envisioned saber, appears and accosts the barber: What was he doing, pray, on that bridge? But whatever happened next, we are casually told, was covered by fog, and nothing further is known. So ends Part One of the story, but not before we have read a description of how the barber usually shaved Kovalyov, which (with false focus) vividly refers to the nose already missing from his face (51).

To Collegiate Assessor Kovalyov, a model of lower-level *poshlost'*, nasal amputation comes as a double shock. For the loss blocks his advancement both in society and in the civil service order. So important is rank to the man that he has usurped the title "Major." (With typical false focus, Gogol constantly calls him this.) Kovalyov is also anxious to marry his way into money. Thus, his dual disaster is made still more acute through sexual analogy. In Setchkarev's words: "A person like Kovalyov who is completely absorbed in his sex life is depersonalized by the loss of his capacity for sexual activity: he becomes a nonentity, no longer has a 'position' in life." [8]

After "Major" Kovalyov has gropingly discovered his loss, Gogol employs false focus in describing the whiskers that go "straight up to his nose" (54). Then we are asked to imagine the man's predicament when, instead of his "not bad looking and moderate nose," he beheld in the mirror "a most idiotic, flat, smooth place." If one ponders the general appearance of human noses, the word "idiotic" seems rather a humorous reversal.

Desperately hoping that he is mistaken, Kovalyov enters a pastry cook's shop to look in the mirror once more. Inside, we read, boys "were carrying in hot pirozhki on trays" (54). Kovalyov quickly reconfirms his predicament. "The devil knows" what has happened, he concludes.[9]

This scene is informed by Gogolian precarious logic. To begin with, the pastry cook's shop may faintly recall the fact that Kovalyov's nose was found inside bread. Kovalyov now becomes surrounded by fresh-baked pirozhki even as he reconfirms that his own nose is missing and invokes the devil. Though usually erased by translation, puns on *nos* ("nose") occur quite often in this story.[10] Here, the phrase "*were carrying* in hot pirozhki on *trays*" contains two possibilities (*vynosili, podnosakh*). The noseless Kovalyov is thus at-

6. Drawing by L. Scorzelli

tended by two varieties of oddly appropriate details (fresh-baked pirozhki and nose puns) as he sadly repeats his consultation of a mirror.

Leaving the pastry cook's Kovalyov sees "a gentleman in uniform." He then recognizes the man as "his own nose"—an eerie Gogolian false focus indeed. The nose, incidentally, has a saber at his side, as did both the real and imagined policemen.

The nose enters a cathedral, soon followed by Kovalyov, who is searching for "that gentleman"—as the nose is called (55). Here, Gogol plays with the nose concept in two ways that survive translation. Kovalyov watches "the nose" hide "his face" in his collar. Then, after awkwardly approaching the nose, he tells him: "You ought to know your place." But the nose soon declares to Kovalyov that "there can be no close relationship between us" (56).

The nose resumes praying, Kovalyov, totally confused, notices a lovely young lady wearing a little hat "as light as a pastry [*pirozhnoe*]." About to make habitual advances, Kovalyov suddenly remembers his noselessness and jumps back. Turning to address "the gentleman in uniform," he discovers that the nose was "already" gone—a typical Gogolian unseen departure. Since it was evident from the nose's uniform that he outranked Kovalyov, this episode in the cathedral combines, as in a nightmare, the disastrous impact of noselessness upon his two hopes for advancement.

While humorously failing to place a notice in the newspaper about his loss, Kovalyov is offered a pinch of snuff. Snuff is "even good for preventing hemorrhoids," the newspaper man remarks, slipping under the snuffbox its lid "with the portrait of some lady in a little hat" (63). Strangely enough, the lady "in the little hat" (*shlyapke,* as in the cathedral) reappears just as Kovalyov's noselessness is reemphasized. In addition, the suggestion that an application of snuff to one's face prevents hemorrhoids may be seen as yet another Gogolian tendency to reverse, or turn upside down, the human body. (In "The Overcoat," Akaky has a "hemorrhoidal" face.)

Returning home in despair, Kovalyov finds his servant Ivan lying on his back and spitting at the ceiling. He "was quite successfully hitting the very same spot" (64). Here, if one pictures gravity taking effect, the word "successfully" rather humorously reverses itself.

Kovalyov's nose is finally returned by the policeman who accosted his barber on the bridge. When applied, however, the nose refuses to stick. Again in despair, Kovalyov writes to a lady, accusing her of stealing his nose in order to force him to marry her daughter. The lady's reply reveals a hopeful misunderstanding of his accusation. If you mean that I wanted "to leave you with a nose," she writes, "that is, to give you a formal refusal" (71), then you are wrong: you may marry my daughter immediately. Her idiomatic expression ("leaving Kovalyov *with* a nose") is of course an ingenious reversal in the Russian.

After this, the story dissolves in Gogolian rumor. The nose, it is said, has the habit of walking on Nevsky Prospect at exactly three o'clock. Crowds gather, anxiously awaiting its appearance. Standing room on wooden benches is supposed to be purchasable from an enterprising man "who had been selling various pastry cook's dry pirozhki at the theater entrance" (72). As before, the pirozhki appear when the infamous nose evades Kovalyov.

If, as Nabokov has maintained, "The Overcoat" is really a "disrobing" of Akaky, until his ghost becomes "the most real part of his being," [11] then perhaps the "real" Kovalyov is the noseless one, exposed in a nightmare world of desperate, ridiculous concern for advancement. In both cases, fantastic events, strangely taken for granted, tend to become a "higher reality." Kovalyov returns at the end to the dull subreality which is his everyday life. The waking nightmare finally reverts to sleeplike consciousness.

Notes

1. V. V. Vinogradov, *Evolyutsiya russkogo naturalizma* (Leningrad, 1929), pp. 7-88.

2. Vinogradov, p. 62.

3. As noted above, Remizov has seen Gogol's works as "a series of wakeless dreams with an awakening in sleep."

4. Vinogradov, pp. 41, 47, 59; 41.

As has often been remarked, "dream *(son)* in Russian, reversed, becomes "nose" *(nos)*.

5. See, for example, D. I. Ermakov, *Ocherki po analizu tvorchestva Gogolya* (Moscow, 1924).

6. Typically, the word "unusual(ly)" *(neobyknovenno)* attends an overlapping of two realities. See, for instance, the prophetic dream of two "unusual" rats that begins *The Government Inspector.*

7. Both "The Nose" and Yuri Olesha's *Envy (povesti i rasskazy;* Moscow, 1965) seem to contain playful suggestions of castration. Olesha's counterpart of the lopped-off nose is a "cut-off" (39) cylinder of sausage that resembles "a live thing" when held in the palm of one's hand. But even disregarding sexual analogy, the treatments of these two items are strikingly similar.

Wrapped in a rag, the nose is almost thrown away on the street by the barber, but a policeman stops him. He then furtively throws it from a bridge into the river, although a long digression delays the action. (45–46).

Wrapped in wax paper, the sausage is carried by Kavalerov to a bridge. He is about to throw it down into the river, but a long digression delays his decision. Finally he decides against it, intimidated by a vision of Babichev's shadow (41-43).

Both nose and sausage are preceded by darkly humorous references to blood *(Envy,* 38). When they do appear, each receives extensive mock praise—the nose is pious, dignified and outranks Kovalyov (50); the sausage is great, a beauty, and incredible (40). In light of all this, it is tempting to see a purposeful echo of Kovalyov in Kavalerov (both names are anapestic). In fact, there may even be other little reflections of Gogol caught in the shimmering surface of Olesha's work—for example, the pretty egg-shaped face of an allegedly imagined dream girl.(35).

8. Setchkarev, p. 157.

9. Later in the story, Kovalyov declares that "a person without a nose is the devil knows what" (64).

10. At one point, Kovalyov moans that if only he had lost his ears, it would have been "more bearable" *(snosnee)* than losing his nose (64). Victor Erlich (*Gogol,* New Haven, 1969, p. 86) combines this pun with the "leaving Kovalyov with a nose" pun, discussed above, by offering the following translation of a sentence taken from an 1836 Russian miscellany: "However unpleasant it is to be with the nose *(s nosom),* it is somewhat more bearable *(snosno)* than to be entirely without one." Erlich's source is Vinogradov, p. 24.

I. F. Annenskij has suggested, somewhat facetiously, that the nose is the "real hero" of the story *(Knigi otrazhenij I, II;* Munich, 1969; p. 5). As co-villains, Annenskij casts the barber and Kovalyov: they have abused the nose (for example, by seizing it with foul-smelling fingers), and it therefore seeks revenge. N. Ul'yanov finds that the nose becomes a real person but doubts that Kovalyov is victimized for "having held his nose too high" (*Diptich;* New York, 1967; pp. 44-46).

Revenge, which may be seen as a Gogolian reversal, permeates much of Gogol's work. One thinks of "The Terrible Vengenance" and of Taras Bulba's revenge upon his own son, which he himself seems to see as a reversal—taking out of this world a person he had helped bring into it. The Ivans' tale turns on vengeance; in "Christmas Eve," the devil seeks revenge upon Vacula; and so on.

Gogol's characters often seem, through derogatory mentions of the devil, to invite his revenge, which may range from a drenching with hot dishwater and melon peelings to a nocturnal ride on a witch and death by fright. But can Annenskij's intriguing interpretation of the nose be expanded? Do other unlikely entities also avenge themselves in Gogol's uncanny world? Does the devil's red jacket (in "Sorochintsy") seek revenge for being stolen and chopped to pieces? Does the overcoat help to avenge its own abuse? Does the rake (in the Preface to *Evenings*) avenge the forgetting of its own name? Does the deck of cards, Adelaida Ivanovna, avenge herself for being used by Ikharev? Does the carriage hold and expose the man who has boastfully lied about it? And do Chichikov's purchases, angry at being disturbed, partially contribute to his unmasking?

"THE PORTRAIT"

Having purchased a painting of a strange man with evil eyes, a young painter named Chartkov dreams that the man emerges from the canvas, bringing gold. His dream is prophetic: Chartkov finds a thousand gold coins in the frame of the portrait. He then abuses his talent by producing cheap, flattering portraits and makes a fortune. Finally, the "pure" art of another artist shames him, but it is too late. With insane fury, he buys up good paintings, destroys them, and dies.

Part Two describes an auction where an evil-eyed portrait is being sold. Interrupting, a man tells the following story. His father had started to paint the portrait of an old moneylender (all of whose customers had strangely sinister misfortunes). Feeling inexplicable revulsion, he refused to continue. The old moneylender, who had wanted "to live on" in the painting, soon died. Hearing that the portrait was apparently bringing misfortune upon its owners, the father retired to a monastery. The speaker concludes by saying that his father begged him to find the evil painting and destroy it. His audience turns to look at the portrait once more, but it has disappeared.

The story seems to begin quite innocently, focusing upon a little art shop, with its "most heterogeneous collection of curiosities." The paintings on display feature "two unusual subjects"—a winter sunset ("a perfectly red evening") and a Flemish peasant ("looking more like a turkey cock in cuffed sleeves than a person").

Next we learn that Chartkov "involuntarily" stopped before the shop, where he submitted to "involuntary contemplation." These cheap paintings, he decides, are only a debasement of true art. This view tends to stress the similarity of the paintings, yet they were termed "most heterogeneous." However, Chartkov soon purchases the uncanny portrait. Yet perhaps only near the end of the story, when the painter of the portrait becomes "completely convinced that his brush had served as a tool of the devil" (III:133) does the full anticipatory meaning of "heterogeneous" become clear.

A shop clerk appears alongside Chartkov (by means of Gogol's "already" device) and tries to sell him the portrait. Chartkov offers twenty kopecks. The clerk's excited reply, "you couldn't buy the frame alone for twenty kopecks" (82), unwittingly anticipates the gold concealed therein.

Having bought the portrait, Chartkov wonders why, exclaiming "Devil take it!" which in Gogol's world often seems to invite misfortune. He then walks along, "full of indifference to everything. The red light of the evening sunset still remained in half the sky . . ." (83). This "red evening sky" recalls the "usual" painting of "a perfectly red evening" at the art shop. Note also Chartkov's complete "indifference" to his surroundings at this point. After his eerie dream, Chartkov is said to be gloomy and dissatisfied, "like a wet cock" (92), which recalls the other "usual" painting ("looking more like a turkey cock in cuffed sleeves than a person"). The two types of paintings seem to have subtly invaded real life. With still another Gogolian reversal, Chartkov proceeds to suspect that his dream contained "some kind of terrifying fragment of reality." And after finding the gold coins, he wonders: "was the existence of the portrait not perhaps connected with his own existence, and was its very acquisition not perhaps some sort of predestination?" (96). Each time Chartkov looks at the portrait, moreover, he experiences "an involuntary unpleasant feeling."

Chartkov starts painting portraits which blend the features of his subjects with those of handsome deities. In the first one, he "involuntarily" (104) superimposes the features of a young society girl upon his own unfinished painting of Psyche.

The Gogolian title of this story seems to expand in meaning as the reader progresses. This title (*Portret* in Russian) is difficult to translate, for it can also mean "A Portrait." While the word obviously refers to the portrait with evil eyes, it can also suggest that the story is "a portrait" of Chartkov, of a man who betrays his rare talent. By pandering to the public appetite for *poshlost'*, he becomes the same sort of shallow, flat person he paints. Chartkov becomes a portrait, the portrait. And perhaps this is why the portrait he buys seems "connected with his own existence" and why, as he also suspects, "its acquisition was some sort of predestination." In Gogol's strangely reversed world, the evil portrait has invaded Chartkov's life, or rather, his "life" was all along a terrifying fragment of some supernatural "painting." And this, perhaps, is why—when Chartkov goes mad and dies, believing that "all the people who surrounded his bed" were "terrible portraits"—the doctor tries in vain to connect the patient's delirium with the past events of his life (116).

Chartkov entertains the Gogolian notion that "clothes make the man," and as soon as he has money, he hastens to indulge his desire. Purchasing new clothes, he keeps admiring himself "like a child" (97). Before, when Chartkov recalled his dream of gold coins, he was likened to a child, sitting beside a sweet dessert and drooling (93).

Another interlocking detail occurs in Chartkov's conversation with his servant about not having a candle (84). In context, these few lines seem merely to emphasize the artist's poverty. Later, when a flattering newspaper article "About the Unusual[1] Talents of Chartkov" enables him to begin debasing these "talents," we are told that the article appeared "below an announcement of newly invented tallow candles" (98). The casual appearance of these candles thus faintly confirms the end of Chartkov's poverty, much as his snubbing of his old professor on the bridge has just confirmed his resolution to ignore the old man's advice never to compromise his abilities. (Chartkov has just bought, and is wearing, his first rich clothes.)

In an interesting twist of the clothing theme, Chartkov's landlord is said to have a character "as difficult to define as the color of a worn-out frockcoat" (93). The landlord, we learn, had been a dandy in his youth. He had also been a braggart, a bully; he had lived a wild, dissolute life. Now, only a few dull, base habits remained. The ironic reversal, of course, is that the worn-out frock coat, which aptly emblemizes so much of this description, was selected to suggest that the man's character could *not* be described.

Yet another passage benefits from supposedly inadequate description. In Part Two, we read about the various nonentities and human "minutiae" who inhabit Kolomna.

It is just as difficult to specify them as to calculate the multitude of insects engendered in old vinegar. There are old women who pray; old women who drink a lot; old women who pray and drink a lot both together; old women who eke out an existence by incomprehensible means, like ants dragging along old rags and linen from the Kalikin bridge to the second-hand

market in order to sell them there for fifteen kopecks; in a word,
often the most unfortunate sediment of humanity. . . . (120-21)

Quite vivid even in literal, jerky English, this passage develops two
images throughout: bottles and fragments. First, the human "minutiae" appear by analogy as insects floating in a bottle of stale
vinegar. With precarious logic, this image leads to their drunkenness—and more bottles. The "insects" then reappear as "ants,"
crawling along with fragmentary burdens, which they will presumably sell in order to buy more bottles of cheap liquor and wine.
Finally, Gogol achieves a murky revival of all these details: "the
most unfortunate sediment of humanity."

What may be called the main passage of the story is also presented
via the clothing theme. The creator of the portrait, we learn, told his
son that the gift of talent obliges the recipient to be purer in his soul
than other men: "A person who leaves his house in bright holiday
clothes has only to be splattered with one spot of mud from under a
wheel, and all the people have already surrounded him, pointing
their fingers and talking of his slovenliness; while those same people
do not observe a multitude of spots on others who pass by, dressed in
weekday clothes. For spots on weekday clothes are not observed
(136).

Part Two of "The Portrait" affords a general background explanation and expands the meaning of various details in Part One.
For example, it is rumored that the old usurer's money "had a
burning quality, glowed by itself " (125). In part One, the gold coins
inside the frame of the portrait were "hot, like fire" (96). After doing
the usurer's portrait, the artist paints a religious picture in which he
inadvertently gives the usurer's terrible eyes to "almost" every
figure. These eyes, we read, "gazed with such demonic destructive-
ness, that he himself involuntarily shuddered" (130). In Part One,
we recall, Chartkov seemed "involuntarily" to buy and to obey the
evil portrait. And he died in the belief that he was surrounded by
"the living eyes" of a hostile multitude of portraits (116). Similarly,
both the painter's words (he exclaims "Devil take it" while beginning the portrait: 128) and his feelings (of persistent "inexplicable"
revulsion; 129) seem to echo and explain Chartkov's.

Early in Part Two, we are told that auctions "somehow resemble a funeral procession" (118); and the auctioneer's voice is termed "funereal." Part One, of course, has just ended with Chartkov's death. But we later encounter the old usurer's statement that he did not want "to die completely. I want to live. Can you paint such a portrait, that it will be completely alive?" (128). Since the usurer has died but seems partially alive in the painting, there is something almost disturbingly appropriate about its being auctioned off at a funerallike ceremony. When Chartkov studied the portrait at home, moreover, it displayed "that strange animation which would have illuminated the face of a corpse, risen from the grave" (88). And the people at the auction are struck most of all by the "unusual [2] animation" of the portrait's eyes (118).

In this final (1842) edition, the story ends with the disappearance of the portrait. In an earlier published version (1834), the portrait does not vanish, but is transformed. As the listeners turn to look, the usurer's eyes no longer seem so strangely animated. The general astonishment then increases, as: "the features of the strange picture almost imperceptibly began to disappear, as breath disappears from pure steel. Something dull remained on the canvas. And when they walked up closer to it, they could see some sort of insignificant landscape" (445). In this version, the painter's son has just told his audience that the demon's supernatural existence in the portrait may be about to end. (The evil force was limited to fifty years as a reward for his father's penance, but in order to end the spell, someone must relate all this, as he is now doing. The fifty years have just expired.) In this earlier version, then, the two descriptions of auctions as funerallike (427) are perhaps more appropriate, for they may be seen to portend the death of the evil forces inside the portrait.

In the later ending, Gogol twice employed his "already" device to effect the disappearance. When the audience turns to look at the portrait: "it already was not on the wall. . . . Someone had already succeeded in filching it. . . ." [3] But since someone has just pronounced the word "stolen," this narration seems possibly the conclusion, or presumption, of the audience; and the reader is left with a very faint suspicion that the supernatural portrait simply disappeared, of its own accord, for unrevealed reasons.

In addition, the ending is tinged with eeriness by Gogolian false focus: how long, one wonders, was the portrait not there while both the auction audience and readers presumed that it was? (In the earlier ending, we recall, only the usurer's eyes altered before the painting was reobserved.) There is another pertinent alteration, the addition of the following sentence, absent from the earlier version. It occurs just before the painter's son begins his tale: "At the beginning of the story many people involuntarily turned their eyes to the portrait, but then everyone stared only at the storyteller, in measure as his story became more engrossing" (119). Gogol thus added a sly hint, far in advance of the final trick, that the eyes of the audience would be focused upon the magician's wrong hand. And if, as Nabokov has claimed, the final "troika" digression in *Dead Souls* is, stylistically, a conjuror's patter enabling Chichikov to disappear,[4] then surely a similar effect obtains here. It is even tempting to speculate that the story related in Part Two could be a slyly contrived hoax enabling an accomplice to steal the portrait. At the other extreme, there is the very faint possibility, suggested above, that the painting has removed itself by supernatural forces. Most probably, we can believe what is printed—that someone happened ("involuntarily"?) to steal the portrait, which even now continues, almost undetected, to bring disaster into the lives of its owners.

Notes

1. "Unusual" is *neobyknovennykh*, which typically hints at the overlapping of two realities. See, for example, the openings of *The Government Inspector* and "The Nose."

2. "Unusual" is *neobyknovennoj*.

3. In the earlier ending, this device was used to show the people "already" leaving the auction and wondering whether the portrait had ever been anything but a landscape.

4. Nabokov, p. 113.

"THE OVERCOAT"

"We all came out of Gogol's *Overcoat.*" This statement, attributed to Dostoevsky, aptly suggests both influence and respect. What is this little tale, which Setchkarev deems "the most mature, the most perfect among Gogol's shorter narrative works"? [1] What is this "immortal" story, as Nabokov calls it, in which Gogol "became the greatest artist that Russia has yet produced"? [2]

The plot, as Setchkarev observes, allegedly sprang from an anecdote about a hunter who saved, long and painfully, to buy a new rifle. During its first duck-hunting trip, the new rifle was lost in the water: its owner almost died of grief. The "real" plot as Nabokov suggests, is not Akaky's saving for a new overcoat and his death upon losing it: "the *real* plot (as always with Gogol) lies in the style, in the inner structure of this transcendental anecdote." [3] Here we shall try (as Bely declares must be done with *Dead Souls*) to squeeze, like water from a sponge, the "real" plot of "The Overcoat" from its particularly Gogolian details.

Gogol, or rather his apparently human narrator, begins by coyly avoiding any definite disclosure of location in order that no real person should take offense. "In a certain department" worked the petty clerk Akaky, who is also described rather vaguely. Most unremarkable, he is: somewhat this, somewhat that. Even his so-called "hemorrhoidal" [4] complexion tends to blur him.

No one notices Akaky. When he arrives for work, he is as unnoticed as "a common fly" (III:143). He also has the habit of consuming his food "with flies" (145). And when he dies, we are told that "a being" disappeared, a being "who was interesting to no one, who had not even attracted the attention of a naturalist who does not omit to plant a common fly on a pin and examine it through a microscope" (169). The leitmotiv of flies thus helps to emphasize the crucial theme of not noticing this "being." St. Petersburg, we read, "remained without Akaky Akaevich as if he had never been in it" (169). And thus, no one apparently even came close to noticing that Akaky was, in Nabokov's words, "a ghost, a visitor from some tragic depths who by chance happened to assume the disguise of a petty official." [5]

"The ghost's" last name, Bashmachkin, was supposedly derived from the word "shoe" (*bashmak*). But precisely *when* is said to be "unknown," though we are carefully told that Akaky's "father, and grandfather, and even his brother-in-law, and entirely all the Bashmachkins went about in boots, changing the soles only about three times a year" (142). Later, as Akaky desperately saves for a new overcoat, we learn that while "walking the streets" he endeavored "to step carefully and as lightly as possible . . . almost on tiptoe, in order not to wear out his soles too soon" (154). Nabokov terms this one of the "harmless looking details" which "gradually dissolve Akaky Akakyevich so that towards the end of the story his ghost seems to be the most tangible, the most real part of his being." [6] This vivid detail of shoe-saving also interconnects with Akaky's last name and with the apparently unrelated digression it engenders (about shoe-soles in the family). Also to be noted here is the word "almost," which gives the description of walking on tip-toe a slightly ghostly tilt. Still later, when a triumphant Mr. Bashmachkin finally walks the streets in his new coat, he stops before a shop window to look at the picture of a lovely woman who is removing her "shoe" (*bashmak;* 159).[7] The overcoat is of course removed from Akaky's back that same evening.

After telling us about Akaky's last name, the narrator explains at great length how he received his first one. With typical false focus, Akaky's mother is repeatedly termed "the deceased" (*pokojnitsa*) while her decision is described. The rather obvious humor (that the decision could not have been otherwise) also suggests that our actions tend to seem predetermined when seen in retrospect and by a narrator who, perhaps, takes apparently absurd causes quite seriously.

The Gogolian blame for Akaky's needing a new overcoat amusingly shifts from the St. Petersburg weather to the condition of his present coat. Akaky visits the tailor Petrovich, whose wife has the kitchen so smoke-filled "that it was impossible to see even the very cockroaches" (148).[8] The theme of deceptive appearances has now developed into beclouded ones.

While examining the old coat, Petrovich reaches for "a snuffbox with the portrait of some general, whose identity is unknown because the place where his face was located had been poked through by a finger and then pasted over with a square fragment of paper" (150). (The idea of "unknown identity" is expanded at the end of the story.)

Petrovich takes snuff and puts aside (literally, "hides," *spryatal)* the snuffbox. Then, having examined Akaky's old coat, he ominously suggests that a new one is needed. "At the word 'new' a mist appeared before Akaky Akakevich's eyes [another beclouding], and everything in the room became a mixed-up blur. The only thing he saw clearly was the general with the pasted paper face, located on the lid of Petrovich's snuffbox" (151).

This rather facetious focusing upon the faceless general atop a "hidden" snuffbox seems to begin a strange sequence of events. Leaving Petrovich's Akaky walks off "as in a dream" and bumps into a policeman who is shaking snuff into his fist (152). Thus, we have still more becloudedness; a generallike figure; and more snuff. Next, Akaky wonders how to raise the money for his new coat; fortunately, he has been saving in a small box "with a little hole cut through the lid for slipping money in" (154). (Note the odd similarity between this and Petrovich's snuffbox.) Finally, when the new coat has been stolen and Akaky has died, a dead man allegedly terrorizes St. Petersburg by stealing coats from people's backs. A policeman catches "the dead man" by the collar and calls two comrades to hold him while he reaches for his snuff; but the snuff, surely, was of a kind which not even a dead man could stand. . . . the dead man sneezed so strongly that he completely besplattered the eyes of all three" (170). By the time they can see again, the dead man has disappeared, so that they are not "even" sure whether he was in their hands. (Once again, a generallike figure, snuff, and a beclouding.)

Finally, the story ends with the following episode: A policeman sees a ghost who is apparently the same dead clerk. This policeman, we are told, had taken money—for snuff—from two men who had laughed at him. The policeman follows the ghost, who suddenly displays "a fist of a size rarely met with even among the living" and "seems" to vanish in the darkness. As Nabokov has observed, this "ghost" is (judging from his description) the "antithesis" of the dead clerk—the very same person who had stolen his new overcoat. If so, a Gogolian reversal, the theme of deceptive appearances, and the three uncanny aftereffects of Petrovich's box are all featured in the ending of Gogol's story.

We may also note in "The Overcoat" a Gogolian prefiguring of future events. Early in the tale, one learns that Akaky's fellow workers composed various anecdotes: "of his landlady, a seventy-year-old woman, they said that she beat him; they asked when their wedding was to be; they sprinkled little bits of paper on his head, calling it snow" (143). Much later, on his disastrous way home from the party, Akaky runs rather absurdly after a strange "lady," is "kicked by a knee," and is finally left on his back in the "snow" (160-161).

But Gogol's uncanny art perhaps reaches its peak while poor Akaky undergoes the utmost deprivations (such as walking almost on tiptoe) and dreams of the coat he hopes to possess: "he even completely learned to go hungry in the evenings; but then, he was nourished spiritually, carrying in his thoughts the eternal idea of a future overcoat" (154). (Note the ironic tension between "eternal" and "future." [9]) At this point, perhaps more effectively than anywhere else, Gogol highlights a favorite theme: lifelike or "alive" clothing. "Starting then, it was if his very existence became somewhat fuller, as if he had got married, as if some sort of other person was present with him, as if he was not alone but some kind of pleasant, wifelike friend had consented to travel together with him the road of life—and this friend was none other than this very same overcoat. . . ." Not the least remarkable aspect of this passage is the fact that the coat, for Akaky, is still purely imaginary. The words "this very same overcoat" thus effect a rather eerie Gogolian false focus. If, as Bely and Nabokov have suggested,[10] this coat (with its "erotic atmosphere"—Setchkarev [11]) is Akaky's mistress; and Chichikov's box, his wife; and Shponka's (dreamed) belfry, his mother-in-law; then we may note still another connection. Since the above sentence ends by mentioning "cotton wool" and a durable lining, it seems strangely related to the woolen material specifically said to be a wife in Shponka's dream. There is also a connection made between "selling wool" and finding a husband in *The Marriage*.[12]

Here, this (purely imagined) wifelike relationship slyly anticipates what follows. Similar fates befall both Akaky and his almost-alive coat as they "travel together the road of life." When Akaky first obtains his new coat, he wears it to the department, where they both are admired and acclaimed. At the party, both Akaky and his coat are also effusively greeted. Then, while leaving, the now-forgotten Akaky finds "not without regret" his now-for-gotten coat "lying on the floor" (160). Soon after this, we see Akaky himself lying "on his back in the snow," his new coat stolen. The parallel extends even to Akaky's death, which follows quite ineluc-tably the loss of his coat. The theme of apparently absurd causes, then, seems laced throughout the narration.

All this is reconfirmed and blended with the theme of deceptive appearances near the end of the story. After Akaky dies, he is termed "a being who had humbly endured the ridicule of his department . . . but who, nevertheless, even though just before the very end of his life, had fleetingly glimpsed a bright guest in the aspect of an overcoat, who revived for a moment his poor life, and upon whom disaster then descended just as unendurably . . ." (169).

Returning to Nabokov's notion that Akaky is a ghost who by chance played the role of a human clerk, a soul, perhaps, who briefly donned an insignificant body, we find that the fond affinity between this "being" and this "bright guest" seems strangely justified. Both "ghost" and "guest" are born in other dimensions (the worlds of the supernatural and the imagination), and both presumably return thereto. Even in this world their deaths (or departures) seem to touch off an eerie rumorlike chaos of coats and ghosts in a sort of beclouded twilight zone where the "real" world seems a grotesque projection of Petrovich's snuffbox and its faceless general, the only thing that Akaky could see clearly when the new coat was fatefully suggested. Finally, we should note that Akaky's new coat appears to him "in the aspect" *(v vide)* of a bright visitor—the same Russian wording which occurs at the end of "Nevsky Prospect" and at numerous other Gogolian overlappings of two "realities." [13] Akaky's death, moreover, is reported thus: "Finally poor Akaky Akakevich released his spirit." *(ispustil dukh,* 168) [14] Taken in their eerie Gogolian submeaning, these words become a rather ominous and accurate prediction of (to synthesize Nabokov's findings) "the ghost's disrobing"—of the "being's" removal of its human body and its departure to the beckoning realm of the "bright guest."

Notes

1. Setchkarev, p. 226.

2. Nabokov, p. 140.

3. Nabokov, p. 144.

4. Gogol's selection of this word may be seen as a typical reversal, describing the top of a body by reference to its bottom.

5. Nabokov, p. 143. In light of this, Akaky's role as a human copier seems eerily appropriate.

6. Nabokov, p. 146.

7. A strikingly similar picture is described in "The Nose" (72).

8. Dmitrij Chizhevskij has of course noted the often astonishing use of "even" *(dazhe)* in this story. See his "O 'Shineli' Gogolya," in *Sovremennye zapiski* (Paris), Vol. 67, 1938, pp. 173-74, 178-84.

9. In "Rome," an Italian prince discerns in this city "the seeds of an eternal life, of an eternally better future, eternally prepared for the world by its eternal creator" (III:219).

10. Nabokov, p. 91.

11. Setchkarev, p. 223.

12. Still another ingenious Gogolian "wife" is the deck of cards named Adelaida Ivanovna in *The Gamblers.*

13. More generally, deceptive surfaces are often suggested in "The Overcoat" by a Gogolian usage of the words "aspect" *(vid)*, "apparently *(vidno)*, "as if" *(kak budto)* and "it seems *(kazhetsya)*.

14. Despite his "manly aspect" *(muzhestvennyj vid)*, the Very Important Person becomes terrified by the ghost and shouts to his coachman: "Home, quick!" (literally, "in all spirit"—*vo ves' dukh;* 173).

"THE CARRIAGE"

A general, whose regiment is stationed at little town B, gives a party. The landowner Chertokutsky drinks late, inviting the general to see his new carriage the next day. Awakened only as his guests arrive, Chertokutsky panics and hides in the carriage, where they find him, miserably cringing.

"And to the eyes of the officers appeared Chertokutsky, sitting in his robe and bent over in an unusual manner." Earlier, at the general's party:

> Chertokutsky was exceedingly satisfied that he had invited all the officers to his estate; already he was mentally ordering pies and sauces; he kept looking happily at all the officers, who, on their part, also seemed to redouble their friendliness, which was evident from their eyes and their slight motions in the nature of half-bows. (III:183-84)

When the hero's wife allows him to sleep so late, these fondly imagined preparations are of course never even begun. But note Gogol's apparently casual mention of the officers' eyes, to which eyes ("And to the eyes of the officers") Chertokutsky will later "appear" in his final, humiliating pose. This idea extends considerably further back in the story. Inviting the officers, Chertokutsky had said: "Gentlemen, I shall consider it a great honor to have the pleasure of seeing you at my house!" (166). Before this, we read that the hero liked to find out where regiments were stationed and "would come to see [*videt'sya c*—literally, to see and be seen by] all the officers" (163). Even earlier, we learned that Chertokutsky had been one of the most "distinguished [*vidnykh*—literally, seen] officers" in his regiment (162). "At least," Gogol continues, "he was seen [*vidali*] at many balls and gatherings. . . ."

As the story opens, we are told that town B livened up when the regiment arrived; before then, the place was terribly boring. We then encounter a rather long description of this "boring" state (the first tenth of the story). The "boredom" is likened to the misery one feels after a gambling loss, or after committing some sort of unfor-

tunate blunder—a faint, but appropriate anticipation of Chertokutsky's neglecting to prepare for his guests' arrival.

There is also some prophetic emphasis upon extended sleeping
after dinner. The mayor of town B is termed "a sensible person, but
one who slept absolutely the entire day: from dinner until evening
and from evening until dinner" (179). He is also said to have the
habit of sleeping immediately after dinner and of drinking for the
night a concoction spiced with dried gooseberries. As all this anticipates, Chertokutsky drinks champagne, punch, and wine at the
general's dinner; then, at home, he sleeps "like a dead man" (187).

The crucial focus of the story, however, follows horses and carriages. Still meeting the hero, we learn that he frequented country
fairs, to which people drove in "britchkas, gigs, tarantasses and such
carriages as no one has ever seen in dreams" (180). At the party, the
general takes great pride in showing off his special horse. "Agrafena
Ivanovna," she is called—"strong and wild like a southern belle"
(181). Impressed, Chertokutsky mutes the general's triumph by
asking if he owns a "corresponding" carriage (182). But Agrofena is
meant for riding the general retorts. Well, explains Chertokutsky, he
was asking about a carriage that "corresponded" to the *other* horses.
This rather facetious ruse decreases the general's elation (since he
has very few carriages) and of course enables the hero to begin
boasting about his own new one.

The final Gogolian joke, however, is the reversal that Chertokutsky becomes the "horse" that "corresponds" to his own new
carriage. Realizing that his guests are arriving, Chertokutsky springs
from his bed: " 'Akh, I'm a horse!' he said, hitting himself on the
forehead" (187).[1] And when the general is told that his host is not at
home, he decides: "However, we can look at the carriage without
him. Surely he didn't take it with him" (189). Finally, of course, the
officers inspect the carriage *with* its embarrassingly posed owner.
Chertokutsky thus unwittingly acts out his own joke by becoming
the horse that corresponds to, and must be seen with, his carriage.

This picture is reinforced still more. Early in the story, we were
told that the "Frenchmen" of little town B (the local term for pigs)
sometimes stuck out their "snouts" *(mordy)* and "grunted" very
loudly. Agrafena Ivanovna, a similar animal-person reversal, is
taken by the "muzzle" (*mordu*—the same word means both

"snout" and "muzzle") by one of the officers (182). Then, as Chertokutsky's wife awakens him with the ominous news:

> "Guests, what guests?" Having said that, he let out a low
> mooing sound, like a calf emits when seeking with its muzzle
> [*mordoyu*] the teats of its mother. "Mm . . ." he muttered.
> "Stretch out your little neck, sugarplum. I'll kiss you." (187)

This rather amusing parallel completes the series of strangely human "snouts/muzzles" *(mordy)* leading up to the notion of Chertokutsky as the "horse" of his own vaunted carriage, which apparently
cannot—despite the general's supposition—"be looked at without
him." Only a few lines after this "nuzzling calf" passage, Chertokutsky exclaims that he is "a horse." After the "Frenchmen pigs"
and Agrafena Ivanovna, this is the third animal-person reversal.

"The Carriage" is laced with playful Gogolian details. The general's party, for example, is distinguished by "a huge number
[*Bezdna*—literally, "bottomlessness"] of bottles" (180). And the
conversation is "overflowing" *(zalivaemyj)* with champagne (the
verb *zalivat'* also means "to tell lies"). As they drink, the higher rank-
ing officers expose their "noble garters" (181). Puffing his pipe, the
general is said to disappear entirely in smoke (181). (Ironically, this
enables us to picture the scene more clearly.) And as the drinking
reaches its peak, we read that one landowner, "it is completely
unknown for what reason, took the stopper from a decanter and
poked it into a pie" (185).

Just before the hero's wife notices the guests approaching in the
distance, she gazes absentmindedly at the "peopleless" (186) emptiness of the road. Searching for a place to hide, Chertokutsky
decides that the carriage barn will be "completely safe" (188); he
then crawls into the new carriage and covers himself "for greater
safety." These touches seem heavy-handed, however, since he has
boasted so much to the officers about the carriage. A more intriguing
detail may be seen in the boasting itself: The carriage, claims
Chertokutsky, is "light as a feather; and when you sit inside, it
simply seems as if . . . a nurse was rocking you in a cradle!" (182).
Given the final picture of Chertokutsky huddling in the carriage in

his nightshirt and robe, his own image of a cradle seems rather strangely well chosen.

Finally, we may note the Gogolian description of Chertokutsky's wife. Wearing "a white as snow nightgown" (185), she arises, taking care not to wake her husband. Then, "in a white blouse, draped over her like flowing water, she walked to the bath, washed with fresh, like herself, water and went to her dressing table." The nearly unearthly purity of this picture is highlighted by the snow-be-come-water clothing image, which leads to (real) bath water that almost seems unneeded, so fresh and pure is the body of this Gogol-ian beauty. "Broken" phrases like "white as snow nightgown" and "fresh, like herself, water" often suggest a dual or overlapping reality in Gogol's world. Here, two scenes are simultaneously developing. In the foreground, we have Chertokutsky in bed, oblivious, while his wife avoids waking him and sits before her dressing table mirror "exactly two hours extra" (186). And in the background, not quite visible yet but ominously en route, we have the inexorably riding officers (who soon appear as a puff of dust in the distance), coming as invited for a pleasant meal and a look at Chertokutsky's new carriage.

Notes

1. In the Preface to Part One of *Evenings*, a garden rake strikes the forehead of a schoolboy, seeming to drive in the knowledge of its own name. Other Gogolian head-related events are discussed here in the section on "Viy."

"THE DIARY OF A MADMAN"

The eccentric clerk Poprishchin, whose diary we read, harbors a doomed craving for the Director's daughter. Feverishly stealing her dog's letters to another dog, he learns the terrible truth that he amuses her. Finally in an insane asylum, he is subjected to painful treatments, which he stubbornly construes as quaint ceremonies honoring him, the new King of Spain.

Gogolian precarious logic seems an appropriate medium for conveying the strange inconsistency of a madman's perceptions and ideas. Probably the most obvious evidence of such a consistency in the diary is animal imagery. People are compared to dogs (III:196), pigs (199), and donkeys (210). Poprishchin himself is termed "a tortoise in a sack" (204). He claims that both fish and cows have been known to talk (195); hence, it seems faintly logical that Madge and Fidel (the corresponding dogs) can write. "I had long suspected," writes Poprishchin, "that dogs are more intelligent than people" (200).[1]

Birds, however, are the most frequent such image. Poprishchin calls his department chief a "heron" (193), and another man is said to resemble a stork (204). The Director's daughter is likened to a little bird (194); her dress is white as a swan (196); and she is "A canary, a real canary!" (196).

Why? One of Poprishchin's primary duties is to sharpen quills. Especially since "quills" in Russian is the same word as "feathers" (*per'ya*), the bird imagery in his diary seems strangely appropriate. At one point, he even sharpens "four quills" for the birdlike Director's daughter (199). In addition, one of the mad Poprishchin's most cherished discoveries is that "every rooster" has "a Spain" hidden "under its feathers" (213).

Victor Erlich has observed that the hero's name is "lowly and ludicrous" and "makes one think of 'pimple' *(pryshch)*." [2] Even this interconnects with much of the diary in a faintly logical way: a great deal of attention is accorded the facial appearances of both people and dogs. The only specific detail of the girl at Mr. Zverkov's is her freckles (201); later, Poprishchin facetiously refers to "a third eye on

7. Drawing by I. Repin (1870)

the forehead" (206). "And did you know, his diary ends, "that the Dey of Algiers has a round lump right under his nose?"

The unhandsome Poprishchin, who harbors unrealistic hopes for the Director's daughter, is told by his chief: "Just look at your face in the mirror . . . :" (198). "Devil take it," remarks the diarist, "he himself has a face rather like a druggist's vial." Later, Poprishchin insists that the Director is "a cork . . . a common cork . . . the kind they stop up bottles with" (209). The madman thus sees his two superiors in terms of faintly related images. Moreover, the word "vial" *(puzyryok)* also means a little air bubble or blister, and one of Poprishchin's revelations is that man's (disastrous) ambition results from a little bubble *(puzyryok)* located beneath the tongue (210). The oddly interconnected series of facial growths thus includes Poprishchin's pimplelike name, freckles, third eye on the forehead, round lump under the nose, vial-like face, and little bubble under the tongue.

As could be expected with Gogol, however, noses are by far the most favored facial growth in the diary. For example, Poprishchin claims that "only noses" live on the moon (212). Therefore, we cannot see our own noses. But since the earth will soon seat itself on the moon, our noses are in great danger of being crushed.

The diarist's nose revelations are related, albeit with rather strained logic, to his life outside the institution. Just before stealing the letters, he admits an intolerance of cabbage, the smell of which fills the street. And the hellish odor from under the gates of every house forces him to "plug" his nose (200). Later, Poprishchin maintains that the man who makes the moon uses ingredients which cause such a terrible stench throughout the world that we must "plug" our noses (212). And the next entry in his diary closes with the observation that "When England takes snuff, France sneezes" (213). There is also a facetious reference to "a nose not made of gold" (206), and when Poprishchin comes to steal the dogs' letters, Fidel almost seizes him "by the nose" with her teeth (201). With perhaps the oddest logic of all, Poprishchin rushes to pick up a gossamer handkerchief dropped by the Director's daughter and almost "unsticks" *(raskleil)* his nose (197).

Just as the notion of stenches and nose-stopping follows Poprishchin into the institution to feed his mad fantasies, so a focus on female feet/legs almost logically connects his earlier imaginings. In the examples that follow, the same Russian word, *nozhka,* means either "foot" or "leg" depending on the context. Sighting an official on the street, the diarist seems certain that instead of going to work, the man is hurriedly following a woman, staring at her legs (194). Then, as his madness increases Poprishchin imagines the Director's daughter in her boudoir: "there lies her discarded dress, but more like air than a dress. I'd like to take a look in the bedroom . . . there, I think, would be miracles; there, I think, is a paradise which even the heavens do not contain. Oh, to have a look at that little footstool, where she places, arising from the bed, her little foot, to see how she puts on that foot her white, like snow, stocking . . ." (199-200). Here we have, as if brought to imagined life, the same painting (of a man spying on a beautiful woman who exposes a leg and moves a shoe or stocking) that appears in both "The Nose" and "The Overcoat." Also to be noted is the Gogolian broken phrasing. As in "May Night . . ." (which, incidentally, the "dress like air" also seems to recall) short, choppy phrases ("places, arising from the bed, her little foot . . . white, like snow, stocking") attend brief, patchy glimpses of a world of fantasy beyond, or behind, reality. Aptly, the mad, desperate climax of Poprishchin's diary features the effect once again: "Save me! Take me away! Give me a troika of swift, like a whirlwind, horses!" (214).[3]

The story also seems to contain an echo of "Nevsky Prospect." One of Poprishchin's revelations is that "Woman is in love with the devil" (209). "Yes, no joking," he declares. "There, just look at her, in the front row of the boxes, raising her lorgnette. Do you think that she is looking at that fat man with the star? Not at all, she is looking at that devil standing behind his back." All this seems strikingly similar to a passage on the final page of "Nevsky" (46). And here, we see Poprishchin walking along Nevsky Prospect within a few lines.

Poprishchin also overhears the dogs' conversing on Nevsky Prospect. "Good," he thinks, "now I'll find out everything" (200). As one might expect, there are several such ironic anticipations in the diary, most of which develop the diarist's deepening madness.

At the very beginning, Poprishchin quotes his chief: "you get so mixed up sometimes that Satan himself can't make it out; you'll use a small letter for the title and give no date or number" (193). As

Poprishchin's sanity disintegrates, the dates and headings of his diary entries grow less and less coherent. Similarly, Poprishchin expresses a great desire to see how various court customs and procedures are performed (199, 205), ironically anticipating his own painful experiences as the King of Spain. Gogol's most vicious touch, however, concerns the Diarist's desire to become a more important person. "Just wait, friend!" he exclaims. "I'll yet be a colonel myself, and perhaps, *God willing,* something even higher" (198; my italics). Still later, Poprishchin suggests: "Perhaps I'm some kind of count or general, and I only seem to be a titular counselor? Perhaps I myself don't know just what I am" (206). He goes on to cite examples from history wherein a simple person suddenly turns out to be "a grandee, and sometimes even a ruler." Significantly, both these ironically hopeful suppositions about Poprishchin's identity are immediately followed by Gogolian statements that fine clothes improve the person within them (198, 206). Later, the diarist mutilates his own civil service uniform in order to fashion a kingly cloak.

Poprishchin's wild outlook on "reality" afforded Gogol a fine opportunity to reverse insanity and normal thoughts. Shocked by the madman's wish to speak with her dog, the girl with freckles is termed "stupid! . . . stupid!" (201). "I think," adds Poprishchin, "that the slut took me for a madman, because she got terribly frightened." Similarly, the "stupid" maid Mavra fails to understand his new royal identity, but Poprishchin tries "to calm her down" (208). And the "Spanish grandees" (fellow inmates at the asylum) who scramble up the walls to save the endangered moon (at Poprishchin's "royal" behest) are termed "very intelligent people" (212). (Dogs are also called "intelligent people" [201].) [4] At last, the demented (King) Poprishchin declares: "I don't understand how I could have thought and imagined to myself that I was a titular counselor. . . . It's a good thing that no one decided to put me in a madhouse then" (207-08). Not long before he *is* confined, Poprishchin walks "incognito" along Nevsky Prospect (Gogol thus reverses the reversal), giving "no indication whatsoever" that he is the King of Spain (210).[5]

Finally, we may note an especially ingenious Gogolian reversal in the word "silence" *(molchanie).* One of Poprishchin's most frequent expressions, as lustful visions of the Director's daughter encroach upon his consciousness, is: "Ai! ai! ai! nothing, nothing . . . silence" (200)—or slight variations thereof. The madman's "silence" is of course both evocative and eloquent. As Gogol was fond of demonstrating, the unsaid (but suggested) can be vivid indeed. Barging in to visit the Director's daughter, Ferdinand VIII, King of Spain, is initially stopped by a lackey: "but I told him something that made his arms fall. I strode straight to her dressing room" (209).[6]

Notes

1. Poprishchin's notion that dogs hide their intelligence and ability to talk from people seems to anticipate Kurt Vonnegut, Jr.'s story "Tom Edison's Shaggy Dog."

2. Erlich, p. 91.

3. N. L. Stepanov, who quotes this passage (p. 214), comments: "Poprishchin's bitter complaint is illuminated by a dream of some kind of other reality. . . ." He proceeds to observe that this wording "inter-echoes with the lyrical digression about the troika in *Dead Souls.*" He does not mention, however, the presence in both passages of broken description (see also my note 30 to the section on Part One of *Dead Souls* below).

4. In both cases, the Russian word is *narod.*

5. The Russian reads: *ne podal nikakogo vida*—featuring Gogol's favored word *vid.*

6. A similar effect results in *Dead Souls* from what a peasant tells Chichikov about Plyushkin: the reader is told only that he used a "very successful" word, though a highly improper one. But the word may be considered extremely apt, we learn, because even after the peasant was far behind, "Chichikov, sitting in his carriage, kept on grinning" (VI:108).

"ROME"

This story, to which Gogol added the subtitle "A Fragment," was intended to begin a novel called *Annunciata*. A young Italian prince, disenchanted with Paris,[1] returns to the eternal city of Rome. Twice in carnival crowds, he briefly sees the beautiful Annunciata. Then, about to commission Peppe to gather information about her, the Prince is overcome by a late-afternoon view of the city and forgets "everything in the world," including Annunciata's beauty.

This ending seems strangely appropriate: both Annunciata and Rome were described by images of flashing light and shadowy darkness. The women of Rome, moreover, were likened to its buildings (III:246) and Annunciata's beauty has suggested "a magnificent temple" to the Prince (250). Thus, the ending of "Rome" tends to reevoke the beauty of Annunciata even while apparently focusing only upon the city.

The story begins as follows: "Try to look upon lightning, when, splitting open black, like coal, thunder clouds, it quivers unbearably with an entire flood of brightness." Such, we read, are the eyes of Annunciata. "Everything about her recalls those ancient times when marble came alive, and sculptors' chisels flashed." Already we have the brightness and darkness which will characterize both Annunciata and Rome. (The word *blesk,* here translated "brightness," appears nineteen times in the forty-two-page fragment.) We may also note the association of Annunciata's beauty with antiquity, which anticipates her being likened to the "eternal city" of Rome.

In addition, we have here a Gogolian broken description ("black, like coal, thunder clouds"), which often attends the suggestion of a dual reality. When the Prince returns to Rome, he is struck by the "brightness" *(blesk)* of sunlit buildings against a "dark-purple sky, with black, like coal, cypresses" (235). Once again, a broken description promotes a contrast between darkness and *blesk;* the Prince, of course, will soon see Annunciata. And both times he sees her, the contrast between darkness and brightness (*blesk:* 248, 250) recurs.

The opening description also initiates a leitmotiv of the artist and Annunciata's beauty ("marble came alive and sculptors' chisels flashed"). We soon read of an artist with a Vandyke beard. Annunciata is said to stand out in the darkness "all in brightness [*blesk*]." Seeing her, the bearded artist wishes that "such a marvel could adorn forever his humble workshop!"[2] Finally, when the Prince glimpses Annunciata, we read that her arms would "turn anyone into an artist—like an artist, he would gaze at them eternally, not daring to breathe" (248). This idea is repeated. And the Prince later decides (rather like the artist Piskaryov in "Nevsky Prospect" that he does not wish to kiss the beauty, but only to gaze upon her (250).

Despite the truth of Setchkarev's views that "Rome" belongs among Gogol's "weak performances,"[3] the fragment contains a close Gogolian interconnection of apparently random details. For example, the opening brightness of Annunciata's eyes, which are likened to "lightning," anticipates the Prince's reaction when he sees her: "It is the brightness of lightning, and not a woman" (250).

Both the artist and lightning themes are present in a description, fantastic even for Gogol, of Annunciata, which is not included in the final form of the story:

> I swear, such eyes cannot be depicted and imagined, nor can they be rendered by the brush of an artist. Like coal, they are so black, and from them pour lightnings. Her brow, her shoulders. These are the sun's radiance, bathing the white walls of stone houses. Her hair, God, what hair! A dark, thundering night and all ashine. O no, such a woman is not to be found in Europe; of them, only legends remain, and their pale, unfeeling portraits sometimes appear in the balanced creations of artists. Ah, how boldly, how deftly a dress has encompassed her powerful lovely limbs, but better if it had not encompassed her at all. Remove the coverings, and then everyone would see that it is a goddess. Yet just try to remove the coverings from a German woman, an English woman or a French woman, and it will turn out the devil knows what: a chicken. Now, a picturesque head has turned, the ring of a tress, a flashing nape and a fine, snowy neck. Another movement, and one can see the noble straight line of a nose, the delicate end of a brow and three long eyelash needles. And what is further ... but no, don't look, don't bring your lightnings. Read of (III:476)

In this discarded fragment the "naked woman as chicken" image uneasily lingers.

Even in the final version, however, the two descriptions of Annunciata (as glimpsed by the Prince) contain a faint Gogolian uneasiness. Upon seeing her, the Prince becomes "rooted to the ground":

> Everything that has been scattered and shines singly in the beauties of the world—all this was gathered together here. Looking at her chest and bust, one soon realized quite clearly what is lacking in the chests and busts of other beauties. Before her thick, shining hair, all other hair would seem sparse and turbid. . . . Before her legs would seem like kindling wood the legs of English women, German women, French women, and the women of other nations. . . . (248)

And after his second glimpse, when the Prince wishes not to kiss, but only to gaze upon Annunciata, he longs "to look at her, to look at all of her, to look at her eyes, to look at her arms, her fingers, her shining hair" (250). "Complete beauty," he decides, is given to the world so that any person may see it. "If she were merely lovely, and not such a crown of perfection, she would have the right to belong to one person. . . ." This ironic reversal, "the right to belong," seems, however, quite consistent with the treatment of both Rome and Annunciata. For as artistic creations of eternal beauty, both seem strangely immune to permanent possession by man.

Despite Gogol's deletion of the "chicken" image, his praise of Annunciata in the final version nevertheless treats other women quite uneasily ("what is lacking" in their chests, their "kindling wood" legs). "Rome," however, contains two yet more unsettling details. Just before the Prince first sees Annunciata, he is pinned between two men in the carnival crowd, and their conversation buzzes in his ears: a doctor was giving to a count "a long lecture about what was located in his upper intestine" (247). And just after he sees her the second time, the Prince beholds in the carnival crowd "an enema tube as large as a belfry" (250). These two details, which attend the Prince's two glimpses of Annunciata, reinforce each other quite uneasily.

As Louis Pedrotti has noted, "Rome" is "structurally whole." [4] One reason for this wholeness of the supposed fragment may be seen in two complementary reversals: Annunciata seems strangely un-alive, and Rome, strangely alive. As seen above, Gogol likens Italian women to buildings and Annunciata to a temple. He also likens Rome to a "specter" of the eighteenth century (237). Its "majestic architectural wonders have remained," he states, "like specters in order to reproach Europe . . ." (242).

Perhaps, then, the two reversals may be more accurately phrased as follows: Annunciata is presented as a marble statue almost brought to life; Rome, as a living creature from whom the life has slowly drained away. Annunciata, writes Pedrotti, is "no woman of flesh and blood . . . but a work of art, an architectural monument. . . ." [5] And, as he also observes, Rome "embraces" the Prince upon his return to Italy.[6] This is especially significant because in the last sentence of the story, the Prince, "embraced" by a view of Rome, forgets Annunciata. As Pedrotti puts it, Rome is the real heroine of the story.[7] Thus, Gogol's shifting of the title from "Annunciata" to "Rome" may be seen to reveal a typical folding over of one reality upon another. And it seems strangely logical that the opening "brightness" of Annunciata's eyes (like lightning amid "black" clouds) is finally replaced, at the end, by the "sun's blinding brightness" upon the buildings of Rome against a background of "black" trees (258-59) as the Prince, "embraced" by the beauty of the eternal city, forgets even Annunciata.

Notes

1. This change entails a Gogolian life-and-death reversal. At first, the prince is thrilled by the vibrant "life" of Paris (200); later, he regards it "like a dead man" (206).

2. A bearded man intensely observing a beautiful girl is featured in two pictures—one in "The Nose" and one in "The Overcoat."

3. Setchkarev, p. 229.

4. Louis Pedrotti, "Love in Gogol's 'Rome,'" in *California Slavic Studies*, Volume VI, Berkeley, 1971, p. 20.

5. Pedrotti, p. 25. Pedrotti also finds "something of breast fixation in

Gogol's rapturous eulogies of the dome in his article on architecture." (p. 26). The article is called "About the Architecture of the Present Time" (VIII:56-57).

6. Pedrotti, p. 23.

7. Pedrotti, p. 22.

CHAPTER 5

Plays

THE GOVERNMENT INSPECTOR

The Gogolian title of this play is at once both accurate and misleading. Mistaken for the Inspector traveling incognito, a lowly official who has lost all his money is wined, dined, and abundantly bribed by the officials of a small town. Tearing himself away from the mayor's wife and daughter, he rushes off just before the announced arrival of (presumably) the real Inspector.

The mayor opens the play by announcing to the officials of the town: "a Government Inspector is coming to see us." Gogol thus establishes a picture of the Inspector "on his way"—a fitting backdrop for the entire play. The mayor then declares:

> I seemed to foresee it: all night I dreamed of these two unusual rats. Really, I've never seen the likes of them: black, of an unnatural size; They came, sniffed awhile, and went away completely. (IV:11)

Diverted by the dramatic announcement that *one* Inspector is coming, we are apt to miss this preview of Khlestakov and his servant

Osip. For they are "two unusual [*neobyknovennye*] rats" indeed, produced by local imagination. As V. G. Belinsky has put it, the mayor's dream releases a series of specters which then comprise the reality of the play.[1] Magnified by the townspeople's fright ("of an unnatural size!"), these unusual rats do come, sniff awhile, and then vanish. This dream is virtually the entire play. Perhaps the most subtle touch of Gogol's trick is the phrase "I seemed to foresee it," which leads us to believe that the prophecy has already been fulfilled (by the mere news that the Inspector is coming). Note also that the mayor announces his prophetic dream as the play opens, to a gathering of all the people it could warn, and none of them ever realizes this.

The mayor goes on to read from a letter he has just received.

> Since I know that you, like everyone else, have a few little sins to hide, because you are an intelligent person and do not wish to lose what is swimming in your hands . . . I advise you to take precautions, because he might arrive at any hour, if only he has not arrived already and is not living somewhere incognito. . . .

Despite this warning, of course, the officials of the town will expend great efforts "to lose what is swimming in their hands" as they desperately force bribes upon Khlestakov. Also ironically, the phrase "he might arrive at any hour" acquires greater and greater accuracy throughout the play. Note also the faintly playful Gogolian negation.

As Scene Two opens, the postmaster arrives and asks if "some sort of official is coming" (again, the Inspector is pictured "on his way"). The postmaster pretends that his sole source of information is Bobchinsky. Later, however, when advised by the mayor to open the mail and read it (as a precautionary measure), the postmaster reveals that he already does this. It is so interesting and "informative," he tells the mayor. "It's such a pity that you don't read the letters. Just recently a lieutenant was writing to his friend and describing a ball most playfully . . ." (17). Act Five, of course, will feature the reading of Khlestakov's outrageously "playful" letter "to his friend," which the mayor "should very much have read" and which contains many "admirable" and "informative" passages. Here, the postmaster even offers to read one letter, which contains, he says, such phrases as "life flows along celestially: many ladies, music plays. . . ." But the mayor has no desire to hear this hidden prophecy, just as he ignored the meaning of his own prophetic dream. Another ironic touch is the mayor's initial reaction to the news that the Inspector is living at the Inn. "It is not he," he fearfully declares (20).

When we first meet Khlestakov, he is deeply in debt to the Inn-keeper, who, Osip reports, has little patience left: "You and your master, says he, are swindlers" (28). Khlestakov then accuses Osip of becoming glad to repeat all this. Thus, Gogol has them both called swindlers in advance and even stresses it. (Similarly, Khlestakov will later repeatedly announce to everyone that he has been mistaken for the Commander in Chief [48].)

Desperate, Khlestakov assures the Inn servant that he need not worry: "the money will of its own accord. . . ." Later, when the officials thrust bribes upon Khlestakov, even dropping money and pretending it is his, these words prove vividly true. And when Khlestakov starts to pay his bill at the Inn, the mayor tells him: "Now please don't trouble yourself, he'll wait" (37). Khlestakov somehow musters the poise to agree emphatically.

Earlier, when Khlestakov has no idea how to pay his debts, he wishes he had been able to hire a carriage: he could have arrived home in grand style, he declares, even impressing a neighbor's daughter (30). As the play ends, one can easily project the realization of these idle schemes, for Khlestakov has already rushed off in a carriage laden with loot and a merrily jingling bell. Ironically, the mayor orders that a bell be rung to celebrate his supposed success with Khlestakov (82).

Addressing his wife in Act Five, the mayor gloats over Khlestakov's proposal to his daughter: "Well, confess honestly: you never even saw it in a dream . . . !" (81). If we recall the mayor's own prophetic dream, his words seem unwittingly ironic indeed. Similarly, the mayor twice emphasizes that he is "not giving" his daughter in marriage to "some kind of simple person" (82,84). Not only is Khlestakov just such a "simple person"; the daughter is of course "not being given" at all. Again, note the repetition of playful Gogolian negation.

8. Drawing by D. Kardovsky (1922)

One almost regrets that the marriage fails to take place. Khlesta-kov's famous pronouncement, "My thoughts have an unusual lightness about them" (49),[2] renders him a perfect match for the mayor's daughter Marya, whose mother tells her: "Some kind of drafty wind is forever playing about in your head" (76). The "love scene" (IV, xiii) between Khlestakov and Marya is thus a meeting of two delightfully empty minds. Their dialogue features amusing Gogolian reversals (of "far" and "near" as he attempts to sit close to her) and "live clothing" (as he wishes to be her "little shawl," to embrace her "lily-white neck").

As we have seen, the mayor's prophetic dream about the antics of two unusual rats tends to slip by unnoticed because only one Government Inspector has been mentioned. But as Erlich suggests, it is possible that the second Inspector is yet another impostor.[3] Osip, who seems to have more sense than his master, urges him to depart while there is still time: "or else suddenly some kind of other one will arrive" (68). If this "other one" is indeed an imposter, he himself may be deemed the second "unusual rat" (instead of Osip), and the play, eerily projected, is only half completed at the final curtain. In this respect, *The Government Inspector* may seem to resemble "Shponka and His Aunt," except that here, the projected "second half" seems more a parallel version of the first. Such an interpretation seems quite in keeping with Gogol's constant use of parallelisms. For example, the exclamations that accompany Khlestakov's detection (*Kak revizor?* [11]) parallel the ones when he is exposed (*Kak ne revizor?* [89]); Dobchinsky and Bobchinsky argue to avoid the blame in words that parallel their earlier clamoring for the credit (19,95); and when Marya finds Khlestakov on his knees before her mother, she utters exactly the same words *(Akh, kakoj passazh!)* that her mother had, when their roles were reversed (75,76).

Perception-expanding reversals [4] in *The Government Inspector* are numerous, even for Gogol. "God himself," the mayor declares at the outset, has arranged it so that "there is no one who does not have some kind of sins behind him" (14). All the patients at the hospital, we learn, "are getting well like flies" (45), a reversal with humorous but disturbing implications. Not only do the "flies" suggest "dying like"; they also suggest unclean, and therefore conducive to dying, hospital conditions. To the judge, who has apparently "reasoned out" some "hair-raising" things about the creation of the world,[5] the mayor declares: "Well, in some cases a lot of mind is worse than none at all." (14)

Reversals are also used in reference to the children of (presumably; 64) the judge and Dobchinsky's wife.[6] While bribing Khlestakov, Dobchinsky makes a request "regarding a certain very delicate circumstance" (66). His eldest son, he explains, was conceived by him before the marriage. But this was done just as "perfectly," he hastens to add, as if the marriage had already taken place. Later, of course, he scrupulously legalized the situation, and now he desires permission to call his "lawful" son "Dobchinsky." The rather dark humor of "perfectly" is thus enhanced by a double reversal: Dobchinsky's "lawful" son, belatedly legalized by marriage, may well be the judge's. The "very delicate circumstance" is therefore doubly indelicate.

The epigraph of *The Government Inspector* is a popular saying, literally: "The mirror should not be blamed if the mug is crooked." The play, wherein the townsfolk blindly force their own image of the Inspector upon Khlestakov, is thus a reversal: The mug (Khlestakov) should not be blamed if the mirror (the imposed image) is crooked. However, both admonitions have this in common: What you see should not be blamed if you expect the wrong thing. Thus, the epigraph is still strangely appropriate. In common usage, moreover, it means: "Don't blame your own faults on others." And this seems good advice for the townspeople, who work so diligently to bestow upon Khlestakov the bribes they presume he seeks.

Just as the epigraph may be deemed reversed, the play itself may be seen as a reversal of Gogol's usual procedure whereby an eerie world gradually invades the "real" one. Here, the patently fantastic world of Khlestakov-as-Inspector is gradually invaded by the grim shadow of the "real" Inspector and by the impending exposé of Khlestakov's obliging masquerade.

In Gogol's later short play, *The Ending of the Government Inspector,* a lachrymose clown boasts a "heart" which offers this "key": *The Government Inspector* is "our spiritual city" (IV:130-31). Yet as Gippius has put it, we have "grown accustomed to disbelieve Gogol," so characteristic were his "mystifications." [7] In the present writer's view, the only justification for this clown's remarkable interpretation is the notion that art can inspire goodness "negatively" (IV:125). For if a "spiritual" shadow can be discerned in *The Government Inspector,* it seems rather less celestial than demoniac.

As many have observed, the play contains an atmosphere of fright associated with the ominous presence of high officials. And the popular saying applied by Belinsky seems most appropriate: "Fear has large eyes." [8] Inspired by fright, the townspeople create their own "reality." But behind the imagined façade, one can detect a faint background of sinister Gogolian forces.

From the very beginning, the news of the Inspector's visit promotes fear tinged with suspicion. The judge (who humorously misjudges the news as portending war) reacts first: "Yes, the situation is quite . . . unusual, simply unusual. There's some reason for all this" (12). His repetition of "unusual" *(neobyknovenno)* strangely echoes the mayor's (just recounted) dream of the two "unusual" rats *(neobyknovennye)*. Moreover, the word "unusual" (which with Gogol often attends an overlapping of two realities) appears at two other key points in the play. One is Khlestakov's famous pronouncement, discussed above, "My thoughts have an unusual [*neobyknovennaya*] lightness about them" (49). Can this possibly be seen to suggest that his masquerade is somehow supernaturally inspired? [9] In Act Five, just prior to Khlestakov's "unmasking," the judge notes the mayor's "unusual" [*neobyknovennoye*] happiness" (84), which words are repeated by another official.

Is there, then, as the judge suggested earlier, "some reason for all this"? Is there any stronger evidence that Khlestakov's mistaken identity and helpless triumph were encouraged by supernatural forces? Early in the play, the mayor declares that if they fail to impress the Inspector, "the devil knows what may happen" (15). Yet, for Gogol, there are not many such references.

In Act Five, however, there occurs (in Slonimsky's words [10]) "a transition from the comic to the serious." As the fatal climax draws near, mentions of the devil suddenly abound. The mayor's triumphant speeches contain numerous devils (seven in one place alone) and even a witch (82-83). When he orders that a bell be rung, for example, he adds "devil take it!" (82), which indirectly associates the devil with a fleeing Khlestakov and his merrily ringing bell. Typically, a merchant explains why he appealed to Khlestakov for help: "The Evil One confused me" (84). The devil then appears in several other speeches, especially often in connection with the mayor's becoming a general, which is of course a doomed plan (88). There are also two references to people having the faces of pigs (92, 93), which, if one recalls "The Sorochintsy Fair," may be seen to suggest the devil's presence in this world.

Finally, when the postmaster bursts in with his Gogolian message that "the Inspector is not the Inspector," he claims that "an unnatural force" inspired him to open Khlestakov's letter. It was as if "some demon were whispering, Unseal it, unseal it, unseal it!" (90). And when asked who Khlestakov really is, the postmaster replies: "the devil knows what he is!" (90)). After this, the devil is frequently mentioned until the end of the play. The judge exclaims, for example: "The devil knows what it means! If he's only a swindler, that's still good, but perhaps he's still worse" (92). The postmaster even claims that "the devil led" him to give Khlestakov the best troika (93).

Merezhkovsky aptly adduces several of these allusions as evidence of "a fantastic haze of the devil." [11] He also quotes one of Gogol's letters asserting that the devil was behind the rumors which promoted Khlestakov to Government Inspector.[12]

Is Khlestakov, then, an agent of the devil? If so, he is a playful and unwitting one, to be sure. Nevertheless, all these associations between the devil and Khlestakov tend to render suspect the reasons for his being so forcefully misunderstood. The very creation of his image acquires an eerie tinge. Behind the comic fear which so stimulates local imagination, there seems to be a sinister force, almost completely invisible, at work from the very beginning—a force suggested at first by the characters' strangely intense premonitions; a force sustained when a dream, a letter, an idle plan to escape, and numerous statements become prophetic; and finally, a force suspected by the characters themselves as suggesting the work of the devil.

Notes

1. V. G. Belinskij, *Polnoe sobranie sochinenij,* 13 tomov (Moscow, 1953-59), III, 456. Belinskij notes (III, 651) that "the great compositional significance of the mayor's dream was remarked by I. I. Panaev" in 1839.

2. As Maguire explains, Khlestakov "presumably means a ready wit or a quick mind; but the expression also suggests light-mindedness, frivolity" (p. 65).

3. Erlich, p. 103.

4. See my "Gogolesque Perception-Expanding Reversals in Nabokov."

5. See note 9, below.

6. "Even the little girl," we are told, "looks just like the judge" (64). Literally, the Russian suggests a "poured-out judge" *(vylityj sud'ya)*.

7. Gippius, p. 24.

8. Belinskij, III, 454.

9. In this sense, Bobchinsky's description of the "incognito Inspector" may hint at considerably more than he realizes: "and such reasoning in his expression . . . and here *(twists his hand near his forehead)* there's so much, so much of everything" (19). In connection with this, consider the strangely suggestive strikings of foreheads in "The Carriage" and Preface One of *Evenings,* plus the several head-related episodes listed here in the chapter on "Viy." Consider also "hair-raising", above marked by note 5.

Furthermore, when Bobchinsky twists his hand near his forehead, he says "I seemed to foresee it," thus echoing the mayor's statement about his rat dream and forming yet another parallelism associated with Khlestakov.

10. Aleksandr Slonimskij, *Tekhnika komicheskogo u Gogolya* (Providence, R.I., 1963), p. 12.

11. Merezhkovskij, p. 178.

12. Merezhkovskij, p. 168.

THE MARRIAGE

The subtitle of this play ("A Most Unlikely Occurrence in Two Acts") furthers the false focus of the title and yet provides a hint of truth. For although there is no "marriage" at all, the play does finally become "a most unlikely occurrence."

Podkolyosin, a bachelor, reluctantly considers marrying Agafya, a merchant's daughter for whom a matchmaker has found several other suitors as well. Podkolyosin's friend Kochkarev crudely arranges for him to triumph over his rivals, but at the last minute Podkolyosin jumps out a window and flees.

Podkolyosin, Erlich notes, is somewhat reminiscent of Ivan Shponka.[1] Agafya, in Setchkarev's words, is "an ignorant little goose."[2] But why, we may wonder, does Kochkarev work so zealously to get his friend married? Setchkarev suggests that Kochkarev himself does not know, and that he, an active man, cannot stand to see the passive Podkolyosin idle.[3] However, since the matchmaker had already served Kochkarev himself unsatisfactorily (V:14), his efforts to arrogate her authority may also be, in part, an attempt at revenge. And given Kochkarev's own marital disillusionment, it seems mildly amusing that he works so relentlessly to obtain a wife for his friend. Moreover, the "ignorant goose" Agafya seems quite convinced by his crude lies. Perhaps her most enterprising act is to borrow sundry parts from the suitors' bodies and assemble, mentally, a perfect husband.

Staged in 1842, the play was not a success. Expecting a genuine love interest and a happy ending, audiences were left baffled and uneasy, as Erlich puts it.[4] All the characters, as Setchkarev remarks, are very limited intellectually.[5] The humor is often quite crude; the comic situations, both prolonged and repetitious. Indeed, *The Marriage* seems almost too superficial and farcical to offer much hope for successful staging. Yet the play contains, as becomes apparent by savoring the details, a Gogolian blending of prophetic irony and precarious logic.

Several statements quite obviously anticipate the ending. As the enthusiastic Kochkarev starts planning the wines for the reception, Podkolyosin remarks that he is acting "as if there really will be a

wedding" (17). Upon hearing that several suitors are coming to
inspect her, Agafya says she is afraid. The matchmaker tells her not
to worry: "They'll come, take a look, and nothing more" (21). With
its three simple parts, this unwitting prediction seems quite like the
mayor's statement early in *The Government Inspector:* "They came,
sniffed awhile, and went away completely." When Kochkarev be-
lieves he has arranged a wedding, he joins the couple's hands,
saying: "Marriage . . . is not simply calling a cabman and then
driving away somewhere . . ." (57). This is of course precisely what
Podkolyosin will do later, after jumping from the window. Finally,
Agafya feels uneasy and hopes that Podkolyosin is gone, at least for a
minute: "if only he has left for some reason!" (59). At this point, he
has just jumped, called a cabman, and driven away.

Attempting to persuade his friend, Kochkarev suggests that a wife
will sit down beside Podkolyosin on the sofa, "and with her hand
she'll begin to . . ." (17). Podkolyosin invokes the devil, adding:
"truly, what kinds of hands there can be. Why, my friend, simply
like milk." In the next scene, Podkolyosin berates the laundress,
saying: "She probably spends her time with lovers instead of ironing" (18). The Russian word *gladit* ("ironing") also means "caressing." Soon after this, we learn that Agafya's father used to thump his
hand on the table—a hand, according to her aunt, "as big as a
bucket—what passions! To tell the truth," she adds, "he crushed
your mother like sugar, otherwise she'd have lived longer." All this
expands quite remarkably the pleasant meaning of Podkolyosin's
words, "what kinds of hands there can be." [6] In Russian, moreover,
the word *strasti* ("passions") also means "horrors" in colloquial
usage, which play of meaning sustains the reversal of "caressing" (by
laundress and hypothetical wife) to "crushing" by husband.

The hand theme is further developed when Agafya decides to
"draw lots" to determine her fate. Writing each suitor's name on a
slip of paper, she tries to draw one from her reticule but retrieves
them all (37). Later, however, after she has decided upon Podkolyosin, Agafya seems to see him "standing" before her wherever she
turns: "Whether I wind yarn or sew my reticule, he keeps crawling
into my hand" (55). Finally, after Kochkarev has joined the couple's
hands, Podkolyosin says to Agafya: "What a beautiful hand! Why is
it, my dear, that you have such a beautiful hand?" (57).

Of one suitor (Starikov), Agafya protests: "I don't want him! He has a beard: whenever he eats, everything will run down his beard. No, no I don't want him!" (21). *(Starik* means "old man" in Russian.) This uneasy image of slobbering may be related to the leitmotiv of spitting in *The Marriage.* Agafya's father, we are told, used to thump on the table, shouting he would spit on anyone who was ashamed to be a merchant (20). Then, when Agafya objects to the name of one of her suitors *(Yaichnitsa—*"fried eggs; omelet"), the matchmaker replies that some names in Russia are enough to make one spit (23). Later, Yaichnitsa is interrupted while proposing to Agafya, and he spits vehemently (41).

Kochkarev, however, is the one who focuses most of the spitting. Persuading Agafya to accept Podkolyosin, he recommends that she tell the other suitors: "Be gone, fools!" But they will get angry, she objects. What of it?—says Kochkarev—the worst they can do is "spit in your eyes." "There, you see!" exclaims Agafya. Kochkarev then explains that many people have been spat upon, and that the chief of a man who requested a raise once "spat in his very face," though he did grant the raise. "So what of it, if someone spits?" (39-40). All this anticipates what Agafya's aunt tells Kochkarev at the end of the play: "For this sir, I'll spit in your face if you are an honest man." (Podkolyosin's escape has just been discovered.)

Early in the play, Podkolyosin exclaims what a "troublesome, devil take it, thing marriage is!" (12). Such broken phrasing, in Gogol's world, often attends an overlapping of realities, and here, the devil is featured.[7] Just before this, Podkolyosin remarks: "It seems that boots are an empty thing . . ." (11). He goes on to stress the importance in good society of handsome boots. Somewhat later, he tells the forceful matchmaker: "Possibly you think that marriage is just like 'Hey, Stepan, give me my boots!' Pulled on the feet, and then walked away?" (14). This phrasing *(da i poshël)* resembles Kochkarev's, later, when he claims that marriage is not just calling a cabman and driving away *(da i poekhal).* These three "definitions" of marriage are thus all subtly connected. Kochkarev, moreover, points out a "dirty boot" in Podkolyosin's apartment as evidence that the latter should marry. Finally, if one recalls Shponka's dream, wherein marriage is likened to "hopping on one leg," the reference here to pulling boots on one's feet seems strangely consistent. And since the same word is used for both "foot" and "leg" in Russian, we may even connect Kochkarev's amusing confusion about whether someone "got married" or "broke a leg" (32). Much later, when Podkolyosin seeks to avoid a "decisive" meeting with Agafya, the overzealous Kochkarev tells him: "Go on, go on, and may you break your leg right away" (54). He goes on to wish him trouble from a "drunken cabman," which of course unwittingly anticipates Podkolyosin's escape.

Gogol was fond of demonstrating two ironies in verbal communication: the frequent inaccuracy of seemingly precise articulation, and the strangely evocative power of the unsaid. While praising, to Agafya, her various suitors, the matchmaker amusingly calls them "so fine" *(takoj slavnyj)* for diverse and even contradictory reasons. Of Yaichnitsa (whose last name she temporarily withholds), she proudly relates that when told the size of Agafya's dowry, he exclaimed: "You lie, daughter of a dog!" (22). And to this, she continues, he added "a little word of the sort it would be improper to tell you. I instantly understood: well, this must be an important gentleman." (The effect resembles that in *Dead Souls,* where a peasant uses an also revealed, but also eloquent, word to describe Plyushkin.) Here, Podkolyosin has already noted that persons of high rank must observe in matters of dress "what is called . . . well, I've forgotten the word! A good word too, but I've forgotten it" (10). He goes on to stress the Gogolian idea that clothes are most important factors in differentiating people.

Gogol's favored notion that "clothes make the man" may be seen as part of his general fascination for deceptive appearances. In *The Marriage,* Kochkarev disparages the "stone house" in Agafya's dowry by informing the mercenary Yaichnitsa that its walls are stuffed with "all sorts of garbage" (42).

The play also exemplifies Gogol's devices of false focus and ironic reversal. Early in Act One, for example, Kochkarev indignantly asks the reticent bachelor Podkolyosin: "Don't you like married life, or something?" (17). While introducing himself to Agafya and her aunt, the suitor Zhevakin vividly describes another Zhevakin, the one he is not (31). And when Agafya deals out cards to predict who her husband will be, the aunt insists that the king of clubs signifies the merchant Starikov. "There is no other king of clubs," says she.

This false focus then turns into ironic reversal as Agafya replies that "the king of clubs here means a nobleman. A merchant is far from being a king of clubs" (20).

In *The Marriage* Gogol indulged his fondness for hidden audiences no less than four times. When the suitors arrive to see Agafya, she retires to change clothes, and they try to peek through the keyhole into her bedroom. Kochkarev is especially persistent, but tells the other "gentlemen," as he (reversely) calls them, that "One cannot even make out what is showing white there: a woman or a pillow" (30). This mildly humorous confusion contains some precarious logic. For Yaichnitsa has recently feared deception in Agafya's dowry: "Right now, they promise houses and carriages, but when you marry, you only get feather beds and more feather beds" (26).

Early in Act Two, Kochkarev overhears Agafya drawing lots and musing out loud about her suitors. Zhevakin, whom Kochkarev gets rid of by promising to praise him to Agafya, sneaks back and over-hears, instead a torrent of abuse. Finally, Kochkarev slips in and stands behind the faltering Podkolyosin, whom he all but forces to propose. All these Gogolian hidden audiences are especially appro-priate in *The Marriage,* because Scene Twenty-one of Act Two is almost entirely a long monologue by the increasingly desperate Podkolyosin. As he, alone, ponders his trapped situation [8] (even-tually deciding to jump out the window), we, the audience, become the same sort of concealed spectators we have been watching, and in that sense, we seem almost to participate in the play. More gener-ally, of course, Gogolian reality takes on a typically two-fold aspect, with the faint suggestion that other eyes, and other forces, lurk in the background.

Notes

1. Erlich, p. 100. Also, the substitution of "selling wool" (V:32) for finding a husband resembles the "woolen material" which is a wife in Shponka's dream.

2. Setchkarev, p. 177.

3. *Ibid.,* p. 176.

4. Erlich, p. 100.

5. Setchkarev, p. 177.

6. The reversed effect resembles that of "what this street does not shine with" ("Nevsky") and of "what buildings it doesn't have" ("Ivans").

7. The devil is mentioned about twenty times in the play.

8. This echoes the opening lines of the play, when Podkolyosin also ponders marriage in a soliloquy, the main difference being that now, when he is supposedly so close to a wedding, he has actually moved farther away from it.

THE GAMBLERS

A seasoned card sharp, Ikharev, arrives at an inn with his marked decks. Hoping to cheat some other gamblers, he bribes a servant to supply one of his marked decks for a card game. Recognizing Ikharev's "fine art," the other gamblers propose joining forces. Using Ikharev's cards, they all win 200,000 rubles from Glov, whose father, a landowner, is mortgaging his estate for this amount. Ikharev gives his new friends 80,000 rubles (which they claim to need for a gambling opportunity elsewhere) in exchange for the mortgage note. The note can be turned into cash only in a few days, and Ikharev plans to meet the other gamblers later. Finally, Glov reveals that he was posing as a landowner's son and that the gamblers have left without paying him, stealing Ikharev's 80,000 at the same time.

Thus, the title of this dramatic fragment (twenty-five scenes) typically encourages false expectations: the ultimate swindle is peripheral to the gambling. Of course, we soon suspect that smug Ikharev will be cheated. Yet the outcome is difficult to guess. It only seems quite inevitable, as Setchkarev suggests, "on the second reading," [1] for Gogol has laced the play with especially numerous prophetic ironies.

Ikharev, for instance, tells his new friends that if a person loses his self-possession, one can do anything with him (V:77). (As he himself thirsts more and more intensely for a victim, these words gradually boomerang.) The only prey available at the inn seems to be Glov senior (a posing gambler), who is supposedly returning home, leaving his son to collect cash for the mortgage note. Ikharev wishes to engage Glov senior in a card game, but Uteshitelny (the leader of the other gamblers, whose name, with ultimately vicious irony, means "the comforting one") warns him that "it will be a completely fruitless endeavor" (78). The Russian word *naprasnyj* (here, "fruitless") means both "vain" and "wrong," which increases the ironic accuracy of the warning.

Glov senior disparages gambling, and to Ikharev's amazement, Uteshitelny concurs. "I cannot understand," he tells Ikharev, "why you are unable to see into a person" (83). His plan, it soon develops, is to win the father's confidence in order to cheat the son; his words, however, slyly apply to the elaborate deception being spun around Ikharev.

Leaving, Glov senior warmly hopes that they will meet again somewhere (83) and thanks Uteshitelny: "God will reward you" for looking after my son (84). And when Ikharev, discerning the plot to cheat the son, reverses his reproach for Uteshitelny to praise, another gambler declares: "Oh, you don't know him very well yet" (86).[2]

After Glov junior has lost the 200,000, Uteshitelny comforts him as follows: "Don't you really understand how you have won by losing?" (90). This reversal of course seems true to the false Glov, since he has been promised 3,000 roubles for his act. However, since he will later be cheated along with Ikharev, his (false) answer, "Do you take me for a fool?" proves quite true. As Uteshitelny then explains, he was referring to the glorious notoriety that Glov would acquire through his loss. Similarly, Uteshitelny soon explains (for Ikharev's benefit) that they plan to be friendly to Glov until they receive the money, and then "the devil with him!" (92). This also proves true in both the false and true swindles.

The overall scheme involves a local official (yet another posing gambler) who explains the delay in obtaining cash for the 200,000-ruble mortgage note. Warmly befriending him, Uteshitelny asks his name: "Fenteflei Perpentich, isn't it?" "Psoi Stakhich," the man replies. "Well, it's all the same almost," says Uteshitelny, adding that they should all treat each other like old friends (93). Later, of course, we learn that they were indeed old friends,[3] for as Glov finally reveals to the stunned Ikharev, the official was not Psoi Stakhich, but Flor Semyonovich (99). Thus, Uteshitelny's statement that the absurdly diverse (but both false) names were "all the same almost" becomes quite accurate.

Finally, just before he learns the truth, Ikharev triumphantly indulges in a long soliloquy about his winnings. In the morning he had "only 80,000," and by evening, 200,000. "A joke—two hundred thousand!" he exclaims. "And where can one find two hundred thousand now?" (97). His question, of course, soon becomes all too true, as the 200,000 is revealed as a "joke" of a very different sort from what he had in mind. This irony increases, for when Glov reveals the painful truth, Ikharev repeatedly tells him not to "joke" (99). A similar effect is anticipated when Ikharev momentarily doubts the success of the supposed gambling opportunity elsewhere. "Well, where are you living, anyway, in the Empire of China?" retorts Uteshitelny, and goes on to convince Ikharev (96). Later, when Glov junior reveals the deception, he declares: "Do you think I'm Glov? I'm Glov, just as much as you are the Emperor of China" (99).

One fascinating aspect of the overall hoax is that it gives birth to a series of vivid characters. Glov senior is supposedly mortgaging his estate in preparing a marriage for his beautiful daughter. "She's so lovely," says Glov junior. "If she weren't my sister . . . well, I'd never let her go" (86). Uteshitelny carries the fun still further by persuading Glov junior to admit he would help him to elope with the nonexistent beauty. During the card game, Uteshitelny vividly refers to a brunette, whom another gambler had called "the queen of spades," even speculating that by now she is fairly wallowing in lechery (88). There is also a "swarthy" young girl whom Glov junior supposedly plans to "take by storm" in the wild process of running away from his counterfeit loss (91). Especially vivid are the (false) local official's little children, "one now running around in his nightshirt and the other crawling along on all fours" (94). Uteshitelny jokingly suggests that the children are already learning how to take bribes "with their little hands." The gamblers even invent another landowner, Frakasov, who is also supposedly waiting to obtain cash from mortgaging his estate (94).

Since so many of the characters are involved in the overall deception, *The Gamblers* afforded ample opportunity for the use of Gogolian false focus. But Gogol went even further. Glov junior is induced to gamble because he supposedly yearns to become a hussar (the gamblers insist that good hussars gamble wildly). Then, as "Glov" is repeatedly termed "the hussar," the false focus becomes double. For example, Uteshitelny scornfully asks Glov "what kind of a hussar" he is if he fears losing at cards (87).

In some cases, Gogol seems to enjoy having his characters repeat false focuses and ironic deceptions. After his loss, Glov junior feigns fright at the prospect of facing Glov senior. "Father, father!" he exclaims (91). And when the gamblers pretend to beg the local official to expedite turning the mortgage note into cash, both Uteshitelny and another gambler repeat the false official's name: "Psoi

Stakhich, Psoi Stakhich!" (95) Two other examples are the use of "you" (familiar form) by Uteshitelny (*Ty! ty!;* 90) and Glov senior's answer that "affairs, affairs" (*Dela, dela;* 80) have so far detained him at the inn. (He refers to the supposed marriage and mortgage, but his words apply equally well to the business of cheating Ikharev.) Perhaps the most unusual false focus of all occurs only if one reads the play. For even after we learn that Glov (junior) is not Glov, he is identified as "Glov" nine more times as he speaks and acts.[4]

Much of the obvious humor in *The Gamblers* derives from a reversal of concepts such as friendship, honor, and honesty. While bribing the inn servant, for example, Ikharev twice declares that he must be served honestly (66, 69). And at the end, he finds his own "honesty" abused by the gamblers he had intended to cheat (100). "Cheating is often termed "delicacy, subtlety, finesse" (75, 83, 98, 100). When the gamblers discern Ikharev's finesse at cheating, Uteshitelny praises the "worthiness" of his "art" (72-73). He goes on to observe that Ikharev is familiar with "the highest secrets" of this art and to note "the depths" of his knowledge (73). One gambler, Shvokhnev, tells a story about an eleven-year-old boy who could false-deal so invisibly that his father called it something of a miracle, "improper" as it is for a father to praise his own son (74). And of course the play abounds in ironic references to "friends" and "friendship," as well as a potentially reversed usage of the familiar "you" form *(ty)*, which can be either endearing or insulting. The word *svoj* ("one's own") also acquires various ironic shades (72, 93, 94, 95).

If Bashmachkin's overcoat can be deemed his wife and Chichikov's box his mistress, Ikharev's favorite marked deck, which he rapturously personifies, can easily be seen as his Gogolian "woman." Scene Two of Act One shows Ikharev alone with his cards, exclaiming:

> Here it is ["she" in Russian, where "deck" is feminine], my most cherished deck—an utter pearl! That's why she's been given a name, yes: Adelaida Ivanovna. Just you serve me well, my darling, like your sister did, win me another eighty thousand, and—when I settle in the country—I'll set up a marble monument. (66)

The other gamblers seem delighted by the idea of "Adelaida," and Uteshitelny suggests that she would be a good "wife" for Krugel, another gambler. But Gogolian women are continually associated with the devil, and Adelaida, albeit unwittingly, helps to undo Ikharev as he uses her to cheat Glov junior. Quite appropriately, therefore, Ikharev's final lines, uttered while seizing Adelaida Ivan-ovna and flinging her out the door, are laced with references to the devil.

Notes

1. Setchkarev, p. 178.

2. A similar effect may be found in *Alfred* (V:192).

3. Uteshitelny repeats his ironic suggestion soon after (94).

4. Yet another faintly unsettling aspect of reading *The Gamblers* involves the stage directions. One of the "nine times" referred to above, for instance, is the direction: *"Glov meanwhile runs out."* Not only is Glov not Glov, but due to *"meanwhile,"* he almost seems to have disappeared before we are aware that he has started to leave. Similarly, *towards the end* of a long conversation we read the direction: "*In the course of their conversation a supper is readied upon the table*" (71). No less intriguing, if one thinks of what an audience could see, is a stage direction near the end of the play: *Queens and deuces fly to the floor*" (100).

CHAPTER 6

Dead Souls

PART ONE

In early nineteenth-century Russia, a person's wealth was reckoned by the number of serfs (*dushi,* which also means "souls") he owned. Taking advantage of the gap between census-takings, Chichikov pyramids a ghostly estate by purchasing dead serfs still listed as living. His scheme is exposed, and he flees.

Given to Gogol by Pushkin, the basic idea —of treating dead souls as live ones—was one of several reversals and false focuses. The (prose) novel is subtitled "An Epic Poem." "The hero" is perhaps not a hero. He visits five landowners, some of whom seem rather unalive, and buys dead souls, some of whom seem almost alive. Chichikov himself seems to be a bad man whom people take for a good one, yet his "shocking crime" is perhaps not really a crime. His boyhood and youth are related only near the end. He meets the heroine (who is likened to a fresh-laid egg) by crashing into her carriage. Yet perhaps she is not a heroine. Nor is there an intimate relationship between them: Chichikov is in part ruined because of attentions she cannot quite bring himself to give her. Finally, a character important enough to be described, on the first page, down to his tiepin, is never seen again.

Flowing from Gogol's pen, this "plot" typically dispersed and permeated its diverse details. As Bely has suggested: "go over to a saucer filled with water, in which a sponge has been placed: where is the moisture? In the sponge, not in the empty saucer. Squeeze out the sponge—the saucer fills up. Outside of the details in *Dead Souls,* there is no plot: it must be squeezed out of them. . . ." [1] Strangely enough, these key details are often presented in pairs. The resulting double image, moreover, frequently serves to color and characterize a third and otherwise separate element.[2] Ultimately, the process becomes an important factor in shaping the narration and structure of the entire completed volume of *Dead Souls.*

First, the two main meanings of the title (dead souls and dead serfs) seem surprisingly appropriate in describing the living inhabitants. "Who is dead?" asks Bely. "The peasants who have died? Their owners?" [3] Sobakevich's soul is described as effectively dead (VI:101); so is the Prosecutor's (210). Plyushkin's "wooden face" fleetingly reflects "not a feeling, but some kind of pale reflection of a feeling" (126). Even the meaning of "serf" seems pertinent, in the sense that the "owners" are enslaved by their own passions and limitations.

The effect entails more than mere descriptive ambiguity, for two elements often combine in potential application to a third. The following passage displays this in a relatively simple form (Chichikov has just left Korobochka's estate): "roads kept crawling off in all directions like a catch of crayfish shaken out of a sack . . ." (60). The pattern of scattered, squirming crayfish aptly points up a lost traveler's unsettling bewilderment. But the crooked appendages of each individual crayfish also serve to evoke the roads. In odd sideways motion, both crayfish and appendages form a double image that guides one's eyes along the unknown roads.

When Chichikov enters the district court to legalize his purchase deeds, he hears a vigorous scratching of pens: "The sound of the quills was loud and resembled several cartloads of brushwood being driven through a forest over at least six inches of heaped-up dried leaves" (142). The jostling loads of brushwood suggest a multilayered noise by themselves, but the crackling leaves below enrich it.

The hyperbole is thus doubled, adding a humorous depth to the sound of energetic paper-copying.

This compounded phonetic effect resembles an earlier one. Preparing to strike, Korobochka's clock emits "a strange hissing" that sounds "as if the entire room was filled with snakes" (45). The striking of the clock is then said to resemble someone "banging a cracked pot with a stick, after which the pendulum started peacefully ticking right and left again." Caught in abrupt Gogolian focus, both stick and striking snake faintly resemble the vivid pendulum.

Smilingly praising the Governor to Chichikov, Manilov "squinted his eyes almost completely closed from pleasure like a tomcat lightly tickled behind the ears with a finger" (28). Manilov's flattering words of course caress his own ears, completing a double image of humorous satisfaction. But Chichikov is also busy making similar statements, and the cat's purring pleasure tends to flavor his posture as well. As Proffer has noted, Chichikov is likened to a cat late in the novel.[4] Proffer also persuasively suggests, with reference to the description of Plyushkin's eyes discussed below, that Plyushkin is a mouse who fears the cat Chichikov.[5]

Inasmuch as he is a man, however, Chichikov is a performer. And his humorous proficiency in swindling is frequently reinforced by suggestions of legerdemain. Our first two glimpses of Chichikov's hands in action:

> The gentleman tossed off his cap and unwound from his neck a woolen rainbow-colored scarf. . . . (9)

> In the gestures of this gentleman there was something quite solid, and he blew his nose exceedingly loudly. (10)

This second description is partly from the inn servant's point of view: he feels great respect for the trumpet-like sound of Chichikov's nose-blowing. The humor is enhanced by Gogol's reversal word "solid," used to suggest the impressiveness of a quite unsolid procedure.

Chichikov's initial manipulations of handkerchief and rainbow-colored scarf form a double image that introduces a long series of magicianlike flourishes. For example, he soon wipes his face "from

all sides" with a towel (13), and he continually wipes his brow
during difficult negotiations. While exploring the town, he tears
down a poster, which disappears into the magician's main recepta-
cle: Chichikov's famous "box, in which he had the habit of storing
whatever things he came across" (12).

Chichikov, a dealer in dead souls, keeps funeral notices in this box
(56), and his final escape is delayed by "an endless funeral procession" (219). Nozdryov, who exposes the nature of Chichikov's trade,
calls him "soul" while doing so (172; in context, something like
"dear fellow").

At Korobochka's (her name means "little box"), Chichikov's box
is described in detail to satisfy "curious readers." The description
ends with

> a little secret drawer for money that slid out imperceptibly on
> one side of the box. The owner always slid it out and imme-
> diately back in again so hurriedly that no one, surely, could tell
> how much money there was. (56)

This passage is in itself a feat of magic. Not only does the drawer
appear "imperceptibly" and vanish "immediately," but these actions are subtly multiplied ("always"). Thus, we have here the
magician repeatedly performing his invisible tricks.

Nabokov has made an almsot excruciatingly ingenious comparison between the inner arrangement of Chichikov's box and that of
Korobochka's carriage.[6] If indeed these two objects may be deemed
a double image, the resulting combination of carriage and box may
be seen to unite two additional strangely similar passages. Both seem
faintly, humorously, and repulsively sexual in implication. First,
there is the postmaster's snuffbox, which he opens only halfway,
fearing that someone might

> stick his fingers inside. He doubted their cleanness and even
> had the habit of saying: "Ah, ah, my friend: your fingers
> probably visit all sorts of strange places." (199)

Late in the novel this oddly improper (box) description has its
potential (carriage) counterpart in the section where Chichikov's
past is related. His former employers, we learn,

decided he was not a man but a devil: he would discover things in wheels, shafts, horses' ears, and other incredible places, places no author would think of reaching and which only customs officials are allowed to get into. (235)

Here, we may again picture the magician's hands and their efficient manipulations. And this, in retrospect, may be seen to add a tinge of odd humor to Chichikov's reaction upon seeing the beautiful blonde at the Governor's ball: "It seemed that all of her resembled some kind of toy, delicately carved out of ivory . . ." (169).

Just as Korobochka's name means "little box" (but Chichikov *has* one), Sobakevich's name suggests "dog" but he *is* a bear. (Nozdryov has the dogs). And though Nozdryov's name means "nostrils," it is Chichikov who so resoundingly blows his nose. (In Part Two of the novel, Petukh's name means rooster but he *is* a watermelon; in the story of arguing Ivans, both men are radishes, but one is termed a gander.)

As could be expected, the clash between Nozdryov, a slippery card sharp, and the swindling magician Chichikov is centrally featured. (Nozdryov is the third landowner of the five visits.) At dinner, Nozdryov continually fills his guest's wine glass, but Chichikov deftly empties it into his plate, unnoticed (76). After dinner, Chichikov observes "in the hands of his host a deck of cards that had appeared as if by magic" (77). Chichikov humorously refuses to gamble at cards, and the next morning Nozdryov proposes checkers. Both players profess inexperience. But it soon becomes clear that Nozdryov, whose checkers magically appear in key places "God only knows how" (he even moves them with his sleeve), is unbeatable, so Chichikov resorts to scrambling up the checkers. Enraged, Nozdryov is about to have Chichikov beaten, but the Chief of Police arrives. And so a double image of gambling prefigures the final outcome of Chichikov's risky dealings. For just as Chichikov slips away and flees after gambling at Nozdryov's, so his host's revelations later force him to escape from town under cover of the famous troika digression, which Nabokov has aptly likened to "a conjuror's patter enabling an object to disappear." [7] Thus the performer himself, clad in his gleaming cranberry-red frock coat, appropriately vanishes.

When Chichikov arrives at Manilov's, a digression describing the latter begins:

9. Drawing by P. Boklevsky (1870-1880s)

Although the time in the course of which they will be crossing threshold, front hall, and dining room is rather short, we shall nevertheless try to make use of it to say something about the master of the house.(23)

Nearly four pages later, we find the two friends standing at the living room door, engaged in a profusion of "after-you" amenities, humorously reinforced by the reader's own retarded progress. Gogol's digression, moreover, contains a double image of similar procrastination. The master of the house, we read, had a book in his study lying open at "the fourteenth page, which he had been reading constantly for two years already" (25). In the next sentence, we learn that Manilov has been warning his guests "for several years" not to sit in two unfinished chairs: "they're not ready yet." The ironic humor of both details derives from attention to partial truth. Manilov has, in a way, been "constantly" reading the same page; the chairs are indeed not quite "ready." This double image of perpetual near-accomplishment serves to intensify the length of time then taken by Manilov and Chichikov to pass through the living room door. For when Gogol at last returns to them, we learn that they have been standing there "for several minutes already" (26), each imploring the other to go in first. Thus, despite the humorous procrastination of Gogol's digression, his original statement was quite accurate: the time taken to reach the living room door really was "rather short." [8]

Gogol's depiction of the Manilovs' kissing [9] functions similarly. "Exceedingly often," we read, Manilov "having abandoned his pipe," the couple would affix to each other's lips "such a long and languid kiss that in its duration one could easily have smoked through a small straw cigar" (26). Both the abandoned pipe and the intrusive cigar evoke an oral pleasure that blends uneasily with that of the Manilovs' lips. Smoking doubly flavors the kissing. But there is more: two pages earlier, Manilov's pipe-smoking repeatedly attends the fading of his ambitions. Then, after the kiss description, we see "pretty little rows" of ashes knocked from his pipe and hear him tell Chichikov of a "most excellent" man who "never released his pipe from his mouth, not only at the table but even, if I may say so, in all other places" (32). The picture of kissing is thus tainted by two

10. Drawing by P. Boklevsky (1870-1880s)

concentric frames of double smoking images. Finally, the Manilovs' lengthy kissing combines with Manilov's very lengthy shaking of Chichikov's hand (17) to intensify the humorous reunion of these two in Chapter Seven. "So strong" were their kisses, we read, that each one's "front teeth almost ached for the whole day" (140). After this, Manilov holds Chichikov's hand "in both his hands for a quarter of an hour, heating it up terribly."

The ending of Chapter Seven, which Nabokov has dubbed the "Rhapsody of the Boots," [10] stands in vivid contrast to an earlier double image of humorous bootlessness. First, Korobochka's girl has her bare feet so caked with mud that she appears to be wearing boots (58-59). Next we read of Plyushkin's peasants leaping barefoot across the yard on frosty mornings to don a single pair of indoor communal boots (124). Later, when the lieutenant from Ryazan gloats fondly over his five pairs of boots (153), his pleasure seems even richer by dint of following this double bootlessness.

Gogol uses portraits to form a highly complex descriptive double image in the novel. Manilov is the first to encounter Chichikov's unusual business proposal, whereupon:

> The two friends . . . remained motionless, staring into each other's eyes like those portraits that used to hang opposite each other in the old days. . . . (34)

In sharp contrast, Sobakevich receives the proposal "without the slightest surprise" (101) [11] and even embarks on a vigorous encomium of his own dead souls. The last words of this are uttered

> addressing the portraits of Bagration and Kolokotronis that were hanging on the wall, as often happens during a conversation when one person suddenly, for no good reason, addresses . . . a third person who happens to be there . . . from whom he expects no answer, opinion, or confirmation but at whom, however, he stares so fixedly as if to request his mediation. . . . (103)

Chichikov and Sobakevich then differ so greatly on price that their negotiations come to a standstill:

The silence lasted for about two minutes. Eagle-nosed Bagra-
tion gazed from the wall upon the transaction with intense
interest. (105)

The ironic humor of "transaction" is enhanced by a Gogolian life
and death reversal:[12] the portrait seems somehow more alive than
the two silent people it observes. Less obviously, this two-minute
scene is intensified by the previous double image juxtaposed above.
The first turned people into portraits; the second, portraits into
people. With both processes occurring during the "transaction," the
enhanced composite reversal at last becomes complete.

As Chichikov first observes Plyushkin, we are told that the latter's
tiny eyes

ran out from under his bushy brows like mice, when, having
poked their keen little snouts out of dark holes, ears alert and
whiskers twitching, they peer out to see if a cat or prankish brat
is lurking about, and suspiciously sniff the very air. (116)

Here, both the motion of the mice's bodies and the expression of
their presumably inquisitive eyes combine to describe Plyushkin's
eyes.[13] Yet most readers will probably not consciously realize that
this suggestive description involves a subtle double image of surprisingly disparate components. And all this seems to support
Proffer's contention that Plyushkin "*is* like a mouse who has stuck
his head . . . from his dark, dank, death-infested house." [14]

A similar double image involving inquisitive eyes occurs as the
novel begins. Chichikov's room at the inn where he first stops is of
the sort found in most provincial hotels:

a quiet room with cockroaches peeking like plums out of all the
corners and with a door, always blocked by a dresser, leading to
the adjoining room, where one's neighbor is settled: a silent,
unobtrusive person but exceedingly curious and anxious to
learn every possible detail about the newcomer. (8)

Note the parallel descriptive technique: "quiet . . . peeking" (room
with roaches)—"silent . . . curious" (room with neighbor). The

soundless expectancy of each reinforces the other. Much later, after Nozdryov has exposed the nature and scope of Chichikov's dealings, the latter retreats to his room. There,

> with a door blocked by a dresser and cockroaches sometimes peeking out of the corners, his spirits and thoughts were just as restless and uneasy as the armchair in which he was sitting.(174)

Chichikov is now oppressed by the intense curiosity of an entire town. The town has replaced the inquisitive neighbor. Thus, Gogol subtly draws upon the earlier double image of silent expectancy to evoke a suggestive background for his hero's feelings.

As Chichikov drives up to Korobochka's in the rain, Gogol imaginatively likens the barking of her dogs to a choir recital. As Setchkarev has observed, the comparison is "set up in such a way that the detailed description of the bass in the choir, with his un-shaven chin, almost causes one to forget what is really being compared." [15] And why do we not forget the "dog-man" compar-ison completely? Perhaps, because the "unshaven chin" seems strangely compatible with the fur of a shaggy hound. Nozdryov later appears "with black, like pitch, sidewhiskers" (64); he also has "a stolen puppy" (67). Nozdryov thus combines whiskers and a dog once again. Still later, the "dog-man" comparison even seems brought to life when Nozdryov stands among his dogs "exactly like a father surrounded by his family" (73). Finally, we see Nozdryov the next morning with "nothing under his robe except his bare chest, on which some kind of hair was growing" (83). Even though torn out as punishment for his intriguing, Nozdryov's whiskers strangely persist by means of what Setchkarev terms "the astonishing 'vegetative force' of his cheeks," [16] just as this "dog-man" himself almost seems to grow out of Gogol's apparently unrelated dog-man comparison at Korobochka's.

Perhaps because of Gogol's fondness for hyperbole, his more sub-tle effects are easily missed. Returning to the dog choir which pro-claimed Chichikov's arrival at Korobochka's, we find:

> By the barking alone, produced by such musicians, it was
> possible to presume that the village was of a respectable size;
> but our hero, who was both soaked through and frozen, was not
> thinking of anything else except bed. (44-45)

Here, Chichikov is presumably about to calculate from the volume of barking the size of this village and, hence, its probable
quantity of purchasable dead souls. But note that Gogol conveys the
hint entirely through vague negation: we are not even informed
what it is that Chichikov does not quite bother to think. (In context,
the reader has no idea as yet of Chichikov's complete plan to pyra-
mid a ghostly estate. At most, the transaction at Manilov's only
established his interest in this strange commodity.) Note also that
the word "respectable" subtly suggests the hero's unrespectable
scheme.

When Chichikov awakes the next morning, the clock that had
seemed to fill the room with snakes does so once more:

> The clock again emitted its hissing and struck ten; a female
> face looked in at the door and immediately vanished because
> Chichikov, wishing to fall asleep more comfortably, had taken
> off absolutely everything. (47)

Apparently, Korobochka's face vanishes because she does not want
to see Chichikov's nakedness. The reverse, however, may also be
true: she hopes to avoid his catching her watching.

A slight variation of the "descriptive double image" may be
noted. Two opposites occasionally blend into a seeming neutrality
that is gradually refocused as one extreme. Gogol's well-known
initial description of Chichikov carefully blends opposites: neither
handsome nor ugly, fat nor thin, old nor young. These opposites
linger in the reader's mind, leaving diverse possibilities open. Hence,
when the town's enchantment with Chichikov is finally reversed to
horror, both extremes remain amusingly compatible.[17]

Setchkarev quotes the "neither too fat nor too thin" sentence and
immediately comments: "Plump, friendly, insignificant, a rubber
ball with a harmless inclination towards swindling—thus this hero of
mediocrity stands before us." [18] The word "plump" in this apt se-

quence surely attests to Gogol's artistically successful contradiction. His "neither too fat nor too thin" hero is constantly, convincingly presented as rather fat indeed. "What a chin I have," Chichikov "customarily" exclaims to himself, "entirely round!" (135). When the town's ladies gossip about Chichikov's being a millionaire, they admit that "if he were slightly fatter or heavier, it would not be a good thing" (159). The ladies even add that "thin men . . . are more like toothpicks than people." And in the final chapter, Gogol rather ironically fears for Chichikov's popularity because: "heaviness is never forgiven a hero under any circumstances" (223). Then, in the section on Chichikov's boyhood, we learn that his "heaviness" was admired by a relative (225). Finally, Gogol mentions the "round and respectable contours" his hero had when the reader first met him (234).

As Chichikov begins his sales visits in Chapter Two, Gogol explains in a famous digression that

> Even the very weather had very obligingly accommodated itself: the day was neither clear nor gloomy but had a kind of a light-gray shade such as is found only on the old uniforms of garrison soldiers, actually a rather peaceful class of warriors except for being somewhat inebriated on Sundays. (23)

Already the soldiers' occasional inebriation tends to tinge this "neither clear nor gloomy" sky with potential violence. Late that same day, Chichikov is caught in a violent storm. And as rain clouds close in over him, it is tempting to connect the loud thunderclaps that begin the storm (41) with suddenly unpeaceful garrison soldiers. Perhaps one can even relate the pouring rain to their drunkenness, whereupon the picture is strangely complete: the soldiers' inebriation may then be associated with Selifan's, which has got them lost as the storm begins. Finally, the words "very obligingly accommodated itself " (which seem so pleasant in context) may be seen to suggest that the garrison-soldier sky is indeed ominously prophetic.

Actually, there are other, more obvious clues. After the sky is described, Gogol continues: "To complete the picture, there was no omission of a rooster, the harbinger of changeable weather. . . ." [19]

And in the very next sentence, Chichikov catches sight of Manilov on his front porch, holding his hand to his forehead "in the aspect of an umbrella over his eyes." Finally, when Chichikov tries to leave, Manilov offers: "Look, what rain clouds" (38). "They are little rain clouds," answers Chichikov.

Sheer narrative space occasionally serves to disguise Gogol's stylistic effects. For example, the story of Kifa Mokevich and Moky Kifovich, which Gogol inserts with such triumphant irrelevance near the end, is actually the final part of a descriptive construction that spans the entire novel. This story terminates with the claim that Kifa and Moky have "looked out" of the end of the book "as out of a window" to help answer accusations that Chichikov is not a sufficiently patriotic hero (245). These two sudden heads in the window are actually remote descendants of the two samovars (one of which has a beard and is human) that look out of a shop window in Chichikov's hotel (8) [20] and of the two Sobakevich faces which appear together in the window, only to vanish almost immediately (94). This strange double image of two faces in a window (first half alive, then evanescent) perhaps suggests that the final pair will be of humorously little "help in answering accusations," as indeed they are.

Bely has noted that the oddly sideways motion of Chichikov's carriage throughout the novel corresponds to the hero's arrivals at unintended destinations.[21] Several of the double images discussed here are viatical; as remains to be shown, the carriage and wheel are both vital to the structure of *Dead Souls*.

The exposure of Chichikov's ghostly estate largely results from the pronouncements of Nozdryov and Korobochka. Earlier, Nozdryov had gambled away his own carriage but managed to transfer himself to Chichikov's vehicle. The gambled-away carriage thus retards the progress of Chichikov's own Plyushkin-bound one. Korobochka's fairy-tale-like "melon" coach later brings her to town with news which helps to ruin Chichikov (176-7). As Nabokov has phrased it, this carriage finally arrives "in a comparatively tangible world." [22] A blending of unpresent and intangible carriages thus strangely hinders the picaresque progress of Chichikov's own, prosperously rolling one.

Chichikov's carriage clashes with another one early in Chapter

Five. While they are being disentangled, he notices a golden-haired young lady inside the other vehicle.

> The pretty oval of her face was rounded like a lovely fresh egg, giving off a similar transparent whiteness as when, fresh-laid, the egg is held up against the light by the dark hands of the housekeeper inspecting it: her thin little ears also shone transparently, glowing with the warm light which penetrates them. (90)

This emphasis on shining transparency is important. When the Governor's wife presents her daughter to Chichikov much later, the girl is termed a lovely "fresh blonde" with "a charmingly rounded oval face" (166).[23] Her beauty haunts Chichikov for some time, promoting his sensibilities almost to those of "a poet."

> she alone with her whitish, shining transparentness stood out from the murky and untransparent crowd. (169)

In parallel construction, the dark fingers of the housekeeper holding a fresh-laid egg have now become the murky fingers standing all around. But beneath the faint humor of Chichikov's ennobling confusion lies a more serious, and eerie, meaning. The almost spectral transparentness of this girl renders her a somewhat unlikely prospect for becoming Chichikov's wife—a concept which must be traced in order to realize its full implications here.

When at last the town's ladies react to Chichikov's dealings, rumor emphasizes his alleged plans to abduct the Governor's daughter. Chichikov supposedly "had a wife he'd deserted," who "had written a very moving letter to the Governor" (191). There immediately follows a version that denies the existence of Chichikov's wife. As this version is developed, the "wife" gradually disappears, remaining in the reader's memory as a vague, mostly erased image. But all this has happened before. A greedy and joyous Plyushkin first presumes the existence of Chichikov's wife by showering blessings on his children (123). Later, Plyushkin considers giving Chichikov his silver pocket watch "to impress his fiancée" (130).

Chichikov's "wife" has thus been presumed and then denied in two separate instances before he finally becomes ill and stays in his hotel room for two or three days "so as not to end his life, God forbid, without descendants" (211). His personal projection of a presumed wife into the future is thus uneasily tinged by the double disappearance of his two previous ones. And the spectral transparent-faced girl seems even less likely a prospect, despite the two strange crossings of their separate paths.

All this is followed by yet another double denial of Chichikov's "wife." Chichikov, we learn, had previously obtained a promotion by almost promising to marry an official's daughter. The promotion, of course, killed the proposal (230). After this, we read that just before the novel began Chichikov "had been thinking of much that was pleasant, of a woman, of a nursery, and a smile would follow such thoughts" (234). Then, in his attempts to rationalize dealing in dead souls, he repeatedly wonders what his children will say if he leaves them no fortune (238). But by this point in the narration his scheme has already been attempted and detected; the hypothetical family for which he supposedly undertook it therefore quite typically tends to fade away.

Bely has termed the entire plot of Volume One of *Dead Souls* "a closed circle, whirling on its axle, blurring the spokes." [24] His interpretation stresses four details: the wheel discussed on page one, the wheel that delays Chichikov's final escape, and the names of two dead serfs ("The Wheel" and "Drive-to-where-you-won't-get" [25]). As Bely notes, it is significant that the name "Wheel" impresses Chichikov.[26]

This double image of dead-people-as-wheels forms a faint, strange symmetry with the almost personified wheel on page one. When Chichikov's escape is finally delayed by presumably the same wheel, it also blends into a double image, and its motion contributes to the Russia-as-troika finale.

But as Bely imaginatively suggests, this motion also applies to Chichikov himself: "At the beginning Chichikov is not a person, but some sort of full-bodied wheel. . . ." [27] Bely goes on to imply that even the peasants' conversation as the novel opens (Will the wheel reach Kazan?) can also apply to Chichikov himself. Actually, the wording which precedes this conversation subtly confirms Bely's inspiration. Chichikov's arrival, we were told,

> caused no commotion and was not accompanied by anything unusual; only two Russian muzhiks standing at the door of a tavern opposite the inn made certain remarks which referred, however, more to the carriage than to the person seated therein. (7)

Since the peasants proceed to discuss a wheel on the carriage, the initial effect is one of humorous Gogolian anticlimax. The peasants' quaint speculations (Will the wheel reach Kazan?) tend to obscure an apparent contradiction: their remarks were said to refer "*more to the carriage than to* the person seated therein." [28] Perhaps, then, the peasants' words do refer at least partially, and of course unwittingly, to Chichikov himself. If so, the wheel's initial uncertainness blends with Chichikov's own uncertain course until, when the wheel is repaired, its recovery perhaps anticipates the moral recovery that Gogol intended for his hero. Most important, the double real wheel image (uneasily developed by the double dead-serf-as-wheel image) now combines to characterize Chichikov himself as a wheel [29] in the troika that is Russia, both of them rolling headlong into the future, rushing mysteriously into the temporal-spacial unknown.[30]

Notes

1. Belyj, *Masterstvo Gogolya*, p. 103.
2. Proffer has emphasized that similies describing Chichikov's external appearance work together as they characterize him (p. 136). He has also observed that *Dead Souls* is a "maze" of "interrelated details and repetitions" (p. 88).
3. Belyj, *Masterstvo Gogolya*, p. 103.
While writing about Aleksandr Blok, Renato Poggioli has implied that Gogol presents the living as dead souls. *The Poets of Russia* (Cambridge, Mass., 1960), p. 203.
4. Proffer, p. 86.
5. Proffer, p. 86.
The main room of the inn where Nozdryov accosts Chichikov contains

"all the friendly things that one encounters at small wooden inns, so many of which have sprung up along the roads, namely; . . ." (62). The ensuing enumeration includes "a cat that had recently had kittens," which subtly superimposes two images of sudden appearance. As inns increase, kittens doubly abound. The word "friendly" thus acquires a slight ironic tinge, especially if one recalls that the friendly but fatal Nozdryov is about to appear.

6. Nabokov, pp. 95-96.

7. Nabokov, p. 113.

8. For a similar effect, see the section on "May Night . . ." above.

9. Both this instance and another that follows are treated somewhat differently in my "Gogolesque Perception-Expanding Reversals in Nabokov."

10. Nabokov, p. 83.

11. Chichikov proposes his deal to five landowners. The first, Manilov, remains "with gaping mouth for several minutes" (34). The second, Korobochka, has the eerie presence of mind to suggest that dead souls might be needed somehow in the process of running her estate, whereupon she opens her mouth, sentence unfinished, and stares at Chichikov (53). The other three exhibit less astonishment, but Chichikov himself later displays a similar expression. Hearing from Plyushkin that a "whole hundred and twenty" serfs have died, he: "even slightly gaped in amazement" (122). Chichikov's amusing embarrassment of potential riches thus seems faintly tinged with horror and fright from the gaping mouths of Manilov and Korobochka.

12. As Proffer has noted, it is appropriate that Sobakevich "turns to *inanimate* people (the portraits)" to present his dead souls as apparently alive (p. 89).

13. Earlier it was the pattern of crayfish bodies *and* their legs; now it is the mice's bodies *and* their eyes.

14. Proffer, p. 86; his italics.

15. Setchkarev, p. 193.

16. Setchkarev, p. 196.

17. Nabokov and Bely both stress, and Gogol himself suggests at the end, that Chichikov is actually composed of pure worm. (Nabokov, p. 74; Bely, *Masterstvo Gogolya,* p. 102; Gogol, p. 242.) If so, the worm can be seen to have consumed the entire inside of the apple that is Chichikov's crimson frock coat, leaving only its bright, *poshlost'*-shining surface intact. Proffer stresses "the hollow center of the rubber ball" that is Chichikov (p. 136). In Erlich's phrase, "The rotund, smoothly-shaven Chichikov is a bouncy vacuum . . ." (pp. 139-40).

18. Setchkarev, p. 188.

19. In an earlier version of this passage, a double "picture" idea more directly connects the "obliging" weather with the subtly ominous rooster:

> At that time, the weather very obligingly completed this picture. The day was neither clear nor gray. . . . A crowing rooster, the harbinger of changeable weather, still more completed this picture. (VI:253)

20. With typical false focus, Gogol carefully calls the samovar that is not a samovar "one samovar" (8). Similarly, Selifan sings "a song that was not a song" (42). The effect occurs three times in seven consecutive lines of "The Terrible Vengeance" (I:246).

21. Belyj, *Masterstvo Gogolya*, pp. 95-96.

22. Nabokov, p. 94.

23. The long sentence which reintroduces this girl contains a digression about how everything in Russia likes to appear "on a wide scale." The list of wide-scaled details then ends with: ". . . and legs—the very same blonde whom he had met on the road. . . ." Together with an initial image of giving birth (the "fresh-laid egg"), this image of "wide-scaled legs" forms a most unusual backdrop for Chichikov's only two meetings with the beautiful blonde. And yet such suggestiveness is typical of Gogol (consider the "carriage and box" passages discussed above, as well as the "intestines" and "enema" backgrounds for the Prince's two glimpses of the beautiful Annunciata in "Rome").

24. Belyj, *Masterstvo Gogolya*, p. 102. (Nabokov has noted this, p. 76.) This image occurs in the final troika passage (247).

25. This translation is Nabokov's (p. 101). The Russian is *Doezhaj-ne-doedesh'* (137).

26. Belyj, p. 98.

27. Belyj, p. 24.

28. Strategic placement of "however" *(vprochem)* further conceals the apparent contradiction.

29. As Proffer has shown, the wheel is frequently, and fatefully, associated with Chichikov himself. For example, after Nozdryov exposes him, Chichikov is likened to "a crooked wheel" (Proffer, pp. 132-33; Gogol, p. 173).

30. I have now twice suggested (see also Chapter 1) that Chichikov's departing carriage seems somehow to blend with, or into, the troika that is all Russia. This is obviously difficult to prove, but it is true that just before the troika digression begins Gogol uses his broken description device, which often attends an overlapping of realities. Brandishing his whip, Selifan

speaks to the horses, who go into motion whereupon, we read, they "carried away like fluff the light carriage" (246). Immediately after this, Chichikov's love of fast driving gives rise to the Russia-as-troika finale. As noted above, the madman Poprishchin (whose story more explicitly contains overlapping realities) calls desperately at the end for "a troika of swift, like a whirlwind, horses!"

PART TWO

Unburned by Gogol, the first four chapters and a final one have survived in unfinished form. Setchkarev cautions that on the basis of these remains, we cannot judge the artistic merits of Part Two.[1] Even these rough patches, however (and especially the last one), contain some almost first-rate Gogol.

Generally, two changes in narrative technique may be noted: an abrupt increase in explicit renderings of the characters' thoughts [2] and the repetitious use of certain words and phrases (e.g., the view of Tentetnikov's estate; his and Chichikov's thoughts that the other is "strange"; the color of Chichikov's new clothes; his hemorrhoids; his benefactor) for comic and sometimes faintly eerie effect.[3]

Chapter One takes us to the faraway verdant estate of Andrei Ivanovich Tentetnikov. The "view (vid) there, we are told, is so excellent that "no guest or visitor" could behold it "indifferently." This idea is greatly belabored (VII:8, 15, 18). Tentetnikov, a sleepy-eyed, Oblomov-like [4] individual, lazily lives there "all by himself" (11). And the "excellent view," which "no visitor could gaze upon indifferently" seems "not to exist" for him. Tentetnikov plays chess with himself (11), and only peasants seem to be found on his estate (18). What "guests or visitors," then, does the man have? For some time now, we finally learn, Tentetnikov has had no guests whatsoever (22). After all this, it seems slyly playful when Tentetnikov's "greasy suspenders" are said to be lying on the table like some special refreshment "for a guest" (25).

Actually, a guest finally does arrive: Chichikov. And Gogol four times terms him "the guest" (27-28) before revealing his identity, even though numerous details unmistakably suggest Chichikov (unusually proper appearance, rubber-ball-like alacrity, pleasant head-cocking and foot-shuffling, impressive nose-blowing,[5] and even statements about enduring much for the cause of truth, about dangerous enemies, and about different jobs). "The guest" tells Tentetnikov that he was "captivated by the picturesque setting" of his estate, although he only dared stop due to a sudden breakdown of his carriage. This completes the ironic syllogism: no guest could resist the view; there were no guests; a guest was captivated by the view but had a breakdown anyway. Early in Chapter Four, the landowner Kostanzhoglo asks Chichikov: "Are you an enthusiast for views?" (81). In the Russian, *okhotnik*, "enthusiast," also means "hunter." Thus, the ironic "guest" and "view" theme is carefully sustained even in this unfinished version.

The description of Tentetnikov's past is similarly sly and syllogistic. Are such people naturally idle, Gogol asks, or formed that way later? (11). "Instead of answering this, it is better to relate the history of his upbringing and childhood." There follows a long digression about the schoolmaster Aleksandr Petrovich and the dynamic success of his lax discipline upon his pupils. The reader thus concludes that Tentetnikov was idle by nature. Finally, we learn that the schoolmaster had died just as little Tentetnikov became his pupil. A new teacher then turned everything "inside out" (14).

Tentetnikov is introduced to us as a "thirty-three-year-old fortunate man and moreover not yet married" (9). In school, he had been given "an entire history of mankind in such a huge format, that the professor in three years succeeded only in reading the introduction" (15). This apparently irrelevant detail aptly describes Tentetnikov's life: the "fortunate" man moves from one extended beginning to another. He was deeply upset when the (extensively described) schoolmaster died, but: "youth is fortunate in that it has a future." Yet Tentetnikov's (future) job made his studies seem more significant by comparison (16). After this, his extended courtship of Ulinka came to naught. When Chichikov suggests marriage to Tentetnikov, he replies that in all things, one must be born "fortunate" (33). Finally, even though Chichikov apparently gets Tentetnikov married, one can easily picture him living in yet another less "fortunate" state.

Ulinka is the daughter of General Betrishchev, whom Chichikov visits in order to resurrect Tentetnikov's courtship. The latter had taken offense at being called *ty* ("you," familiar form) by the General, a twist of meaning which Gogol also exploited in *The Gamblers.*) (*Ty*, which can suggest either contempt or deep affection, seems reay-made for use as a Gogolian reversal.)

The General is a widower who "loves his daughter madly" (23). Chichikov achieves success with the General, however, by telling his daughter that everyone needs love. "Even a cow," he declares, "likes to be stroked. It sticks its muzzle through the pen for this: come, stroke me." The General dissolves in laughter. His shoulders, "which once carried thick epaulets, shook just as if they even now carried thick epaulets." Chichikov also laughs, but "respectfully"—his shoulders did not shake because "they did not carry thick epaulets." This facetious twist raises a rather unsettling distinction between the absence of real epaulets and the absence of unreal ones.

Chichikov's words about the cow's muzzle needing a stroking (which faintly recall the bedroom scene in "The Carriage") are happily repeated by Betrishchev. The idea of a cow in love renders him receptive to renewing his friendship with Tentetnikov. Earlier, we learned that a landowner considered Tentetnikov "a most natural cow!" (9). And Chickokov, inspecting Tentetnikov's idle hands, has already considered him "a cow!"(31). This Gogolian double image is especially effective in the Russian because *skotina*, "cow," also means "beast" or "swine." More generally, this continues the people-as-animals theme of Part One. Here, the General is likened to a duck (43) and a landowner in Chapter Three is called Petukh ("rooster"). Like Korobochka's carriage, Petukh is likened to a watermelon and then called "the watermelon" with Gogolian false focus.[6]

Other Gogolian touches in Part Two include the sudden mention of a servant with a towel (10) who has been present beside the eye-rubbing Tentetnikov "all along" (like the inn servant with towel who abruptly materializes beside Chichikov). And Tentetnikov himself habitually becomes a Gogolian hidden audience for the conversations of his serfs (10). Also typically, women are termed "the excellent sex" as we learn of their quarrels and gossiping (20). And Gogol even seems to reverse a reversal by describing a "red-nosed, red-legged martin" walking along a river bank—"a bird, of course, and not a person" (21).

As in Part One, Chichikov is seeking to acquire dead souls, and Gogol has Tentetnikov speculate, when his "guest" first arrives, that Chichikov is a professor, traveling about in search of plants, or, perhaps, "fossilized objects" (27). The word *iskopaemye* (here, "fossilized objects") literally means "dug up things"—which seems a rather darkly humorous manifestation of Gogolian precarious logic. (Korobochka, we recall, asked Chichikov if he wanted "to dig up" the dead souls "out of the ground" [VI:51].)

Chapter Two exists only as a nine-page fragment. Chichikov visits General Betrishchev and arranges both Tentetnikov's marriage to Ulinka and his own acquisition of dead souls. In both cases, Chichikov amuses the General until the latter shakes with laughter. To get the dead souls, Chichikov invents a rich uncle who will leave him money only if he, Chichikov, can prove his worth by obtaining three hundred souls on his own. The idea of duping the uncle with dead souls greatly appeals to the General.

One vivid lie breeds another. Chichikov's "uncle" (about eighty years old, who has only two teeth and barely stands on his feet) supposedly has a housekeeper. This housekeeper has children, who seem destined to receive the inheritance if Chichikov fails to obtain the three hundred souls. (The humor of connecting the children only with their mother recalls the description of Gapka and *her* children in the "Ivans" tale.)

General Betrishchev is a solid old fellow whose neck is fat in the back, "with three so-called floors, or three folds" (37). Ulinka, whom Setchkarev suggests was meant to embody the perfect woman,[7] produces a strangely abstracted effect. She appears in the neuter case (Chichikov is unable to make out "just what was standing before him"). And, we read: "It was difficult to say of what land she was a native" (40). Like Annunciata in "Rome," Ulinka is likened to ancient sculpture (41). And her clothes are so perfect that other young ladies, fashionably dressed, would have seemed like "speckled trout" beside her. (Beside Annunciata, the legs of other women seem like "kindling wood.")

Chapter Three features more of Chichikov's travels. Having arranged the marriage, he is asked by Betrishchev (who has just become his "benefactor" by providing the three hundred dead souls) to spread the news to various relatives.[8] As in Part One, however, a servant's blunder (this time, Petrushka's) brings Chichikov to the wrong landowner: Peter Petrovich Petukh.

Petukh is in a lake helping his peasants with a fishing net when Chichikov arrives "A strange person, this Koshkaryov," thinks Chichikov, who takes Petukh for the General's relative he is seeking.

Since Petukh is also likened to, and then termed, a watermelon, the false focus becomes double. Gogol also repeatedly uses his "already" *(uzhe)* device [9] to have Petukh mysteriously appear and disappear from Chichikov's view (48-49).

Petukh tells Chichikov that he has mortgaged his estate because everyone is doing so, and he does not wish to "lag behind" the others (50). This amusing reversal then turns into a syllogism as Chichikov thinks to himself "what a fool" the man is to squander his possessions. "Oh, I know what you're thinking," says Petukh. "What?" asks Chichikov. "You're thinking: 'What a fool, what a fool this Petukh is! Invited me to dinner, and not a sign of it yet.' "

Petukh, as his watermelon shape suggests, lives only for food, and his customary greeting is: "Have you eaten?" (48,51). A neighbor, Platonov, arrives soon after Chichikov and disappoints Petukh with the reply that he has already dined. The syllogism then becomes complete: when he dined, Platonov had no appetite and consequently "ate nothing" (51).

Platonov displays a bordeom not unlike that of Pushkin's Onegin, as Setchkarev has observed.[10] Chichikov sympathetically, and hopefully, suggests that this boredom may be caused by the deaths of many serfs, but little comes of his inquiry. Gogol, does, however, add two somewhat unsettling touches. Serving Chichikov roast calf, Petukh declares that he looked after the animal like his own son (53). And so lavishly does Petukh order dinner for the next day, that "A corpse's appetite would have arisen" (56).

Chichikov likens the world to "a living book" (54)—a reversal he enjoys repeating (61, 92)—and convinces Platnov that traveling may cure his boredom. Groggy from overeating, they leave Petukh's estate. First they visit Platonov's sister, who is married to the landowner Kostanzhoglo.

Chichikov briefly visits the General's relative Koshkaryov (whom Kostanzhoglo terms "crazy") and almost buys some dead souls. The purchase, however, becomes hopelessly postponed by the red tape of numerous administrative offices set up by Koshkaryov to run his estate. Returning to Kostanzhoglo's, Chichikov learns that an indebted landowner, Hlobuev, will probably sell his estate at a bargain price.

In Chapter Four, Chichikov buys Holbuev's dilapidated estate and its 100 souls, only fifty of whom have survived a cholera epidemic. And these, Hlobuev sadly admits, have no official papers, so even they are considered "dead" (85). Thus, when Chichikov finally becomes the owner of "live" souls, even these are humorously unsubstantial. However, it also costs him even less than usual. The estate is sold for 25,000 rubles, 10,000, of which (borrowed from Kostanzhoglo) are paid immediately and another 5,000 of which (borrowed from Platonov) are promised for delivery the next day, "that is, promised; it was planned to bring three, the rest—later, maybe in two or three days, and if possible, to postpone it yet somewhat more" (86). Thus, Chichikov uses no money of his own and may even save from his borrowings.

In fact, Chichikov soon reflects that it may be possible even to avoid paying Kostanzhoglo (89). At this point we are told that "a strange thought," all on its own, suddenly visited Chichikov, "teasing, smirking, and winking at him." And who, we are asked, creates these wanton thoughts which suddenly invade us? Gogol's technique here recalls the (also unrevealed) word used by a peasant to describe Plyushkin in Part One, which causes a smile to keep returning to Chichikov's face.

Chichikov's purchase also gives rise to thoughts of his future children (89). He has already vividly pictured a wife and children twice before (31, 55), which continues the theme of his doubly reinforced, but purely imaginary family established in Part One. In the concluding chapter of Part Two, we even learn that Chichikov asked for mercy because of his wife and children (108).

Chichikov and Platonov next visit the latter's brother Vasily. Various dogs kiss each other; then one kisses Chichikov on the ear; he then kisses Vasily as they are introduced by Platonov (90; this faintly recalls the scene in Part One wherein one of Nozdryov's dogs licks Chichikov on the lips). Vasily is susupcious of his brother's new friend, with whom he plans to travel about Russia. Chichikov, he fears, may be "trash, and the devil knows what" (91). Distrustfully scrutinizing Chichikov, however, Vasily finds only "astonishing decorum of demeanor."

Chapter Four ends with Chichikov's visit to Lenitsyn, who is supposedly stealing land from Vasily. At Lenitsyn's, the question of purchasing dead souls is raised once again. Chichikov waxes eloquent, but his host remains undecided. The Lenitsyn's baby is brought in. Chichikov entices the baby into his arms, where "from sudden pleasure or some other cause" it misbehaves on his frock coat. "This apparently insignificant occurrence," we read "completely inclined the host in favor of Chichikov's negotiation" (95).[11]

As the final chapter begins, Chichikov has presumably manipulated the will of Hlobuev's rich aunt for his own benefit. When we meet him again, he is purchasing material for a new frock coat. He selects what the clerk terms "An excellent color. Cloth of Navarino smoke and flame" (99). Chichikov had requested a combination of dark green or olive with cranberry, and the "Navarino smoke and flame"[12] cloth pleases him. Soon after, Chichikov proudly tries on his "new frock coat of Navarino flame and smoke." Again he is pleased. "Now to whom should I appear first of all?" he wonders (106). At his very moment, a gendarme in full military uniform, as if representing "an entire army," approaches Chichikov and says: "You are ordered to appear immediately to the General-Governor." Thus, Chichikov's proud words about "appearing to someone become ironically prophetic, and even the celebrated "military" color of his new coat seems to have strangely anticipated his arrest (a rather eerie twist of the Gogolian "live" clothing theme).

The General-Governor shatters Chichikov with the news that they have captured the woman who forged the will at his dictation. Chichikov begs for mercy, even embracing the man's foot. Desperately hugging the foot to his chest, he is dragged, "together with the foot, along the floor in his frock coat of Navarino flame and smoke" (108). At this point, the General-Governor is said to experience the "revulsion that a person feels at the sight of a most ugly insect, which he lacks the spirit to crush with his foot." This Gogolian interconnection of details extends even further. After the General-Governor shakes his foot and Chichikov feels "the impact of a boot on his nose," he is locked up in an old damp room "with the odor of boots" (109).

As Setchkarev has observed, a religious note is strongly sounded in the final chapter, which ends, like Part One, with Chichikov's departure.[13] If the hero was ever to be reformed in a Part Three of *Dead Souls,* Gogol was presumably attempting to make some preparations here.[14] Imprisoned, Chichikov is visited by the religious and influential Murazov (who later persuades the General-Governor to free Chichikov, providing he will leave town immediately). The prisoner bemoans the loss of his box containing money and papers. It is time, says Murazov, to think "of your poor soul" (110).

Gogol pays even more attention to the souls of living people in Part Two than in Part One. For example, we are told that Tentetnikov avoided debauchery in his youth: "his soul sensed its heavenly origin" (14). Compared with the humorous descriptions of both Sobakevich's and the Prosecutor's apparently nonexistent souls (VI:101,210), this notion seems quite unlike Gogol, yet it may well indicate an alteration which his strangely anticipatory mind was preparing for his hero.[15] Just before Chichikov is captured, Murazov convinces Hlobuev that he should work to collect funds for a new church. As he agrees, Hlobuev feels a surge of strength entering his soul (104). When he is caught, Chichikov exclaims that his soul will be destroyed (107), which anticipates Murazov's admonition to think of his "poor soul." Then, as Murazov exhorts Chichikov to reform, their conversation is interrupted by a paragraph beginning "There are secrets of the soul" and suggesting that even the most wayward sinner may be reached and moved. Chichikov, however, continues to plead for his money and papers. Murazov warns that because of wrongly emphasizing material things, Chichikov does not listen to his poor soul. "I'll think about my soul," says Chichikov, "but save me" (112).

Murazov insists at length that only God can save him. "Chichikov, it seemed, felt something with the half-awakened forces of his soul" (115). Finally, when Murazov informs Chichikov that he is free, he says: "the body depends upon the soul. . . . Think not about dead souls, but about your living soul . . ." (123). Chichikov then leaves and buys yet another new suit. Given Gogol's fascination for suggesting a nearly organic connection between clothes and the body inside them, it seems possible that he had in mind here a new body for Chichikov's rediscovered soul. For as he pays the tailor and leaves, we read: "This was not the former Chichikov. It was some sort of ruins of the former Chichikov. The inner condition of his soul could have been compared to a dismantled structure which has been dismantled in order to be built into a new one; yet the new one has not been begun because a definite plan has not arrived from the architect, and the workers are left in a quandary" (124).

But Gogol (rather typically) seems almost to be making a case opposite to the apparent meaning of his words. The quandary seems too playful, too ingeniously self-undermining, even for the groundwork of serious salvation. The humor lingers far more vividly than do any solemn hopes for the hero's soul. His attitude still echoes: All right, I'll think about my soul, but return my money and my papers. Moreover, we may recall Chichikov's amusing explanation to Murazov that he was "crooked only when the straight path could not be taken and the crooked one was more direct" (111). Given Gogol's reverse vision, to be saved was perhaps dangerously close to being damned, and if Chichikov was indeed supposed to be resurrected, there seems little surviving evidence that this had ever been convincingly accomplished by Nikolai Gogol.

Notes

1. Setchkarev, p. 248.

2. See especially VII:34-35,86.

3. Proffer has observed that Part Two "is filled with repetitions and redundancies of all kinds," and he quotes Gippius on Gogol's attempts to show the mental evolution of his characters (pp. 155-56).

4. See Setchkarev, p. 249; Erlich, p. 173.

5. As Proffer notes, Chichikov's name suggests the Russian word *chikhat'*, "to sneeze" (p. 88).

6. See Proffer, pp. 83, 165.

7. Setchkarev, p. 249.

8. Setchkarev explains this on the basis of other sources (p. 250).

9. Later in the chapter, the word *uzhe* appears five times in five consecutive sentences to set the scene as the landowners return from a boat ride (55).

10. Setchkarev, p. 250.

11. See the discussions of apparently insignificant, and apparently absurd, causes here in the chapters on "Old World Landowners" and "The Overcoat," respectively.

12. Maguire notes that "Navarino was an important naval battle (October 20, 1827) in the War of Greek Independence" (p. 79).

13. Setchkarev, p. 252.

14. As Setchkarev observes, however, Chichikov is again indirectly identified with the antichrist (p. 253); Gogol, p. 118.

15. Proffer has suggested that Gogol views several characters (in Part One of *Dead Souls*) as having hidden souls awaiting liberation (p. 104).

Conclusion

Gogol's creative works, like the writings of the Russian Symbolists, some of whom fervently returned to him,[1] may be seen as an effort to reach beyond the limitations of words, thoughts, and normal conscious perception. But with Gogol, it seems to have been less of an effort. Whether or not one agrees that his impulses were inspired either divinely or diabolically,[2] Gogol's own brand of Romanticism predicates three basic characteristics or techniques: reverse vision, false focus and precarious logic. Especially these three elements of his art generated its strangely expanding quality. They enabled him to go—or at least to create the illusion of going—beyond words with words. His writing, as Nabokov has suggested, "gives one the sensation of something ludicrous and at the same time stellar." [3]

Helen Muchnic has gathered Gogol, Poe, and Baudelaire together under Hegel's term "The Unhappy Consciousness," which, she writes, accepts neither "the certitude of negation, nor the flight from the objects of perception." [4] Perhaps we could say that Gogol's writing evinces a flight *beyond* the objects of perception. The retreat is a strangely aggressive one.

At first misunderstood as a realist, Gogol has also been widely, and wrongly, considered a writer of tales that should make one's "flesh creep" or make one "rock with laughter." [5] But Nikolai Gogol did not produce merely scary or comic stories.[6] His "tomfoolery," as Muchnic suggests, is more than that: Gogol is "masking anxiety in a huge joke about something too vague and terrible to be talked about openly." [7] The reader's "laugh" is often a rather uneasy one. And the "flesh creeping" effect, if such it may be called, is oddly exhilarating. One's experience, however uneasy, contains an element of relief. It could even be said to free the reader, at least momentarily, from the guilt of accepting the too familiar limitations of everyday conscious perception.

As traced by the present study, Gogolian reverse vision may be assigned to three general areas: chronology, morality, and reality. Joseph Frank has demonstrated how Flaubert solved the problem of presenting separate scenes as happening simultaneously. Flaubert, he explains, moves his focus back and forth until, at the climax, key words from different scenes "are read at almost the same moment." [8] Gogol employed a similar (though less interwoven) technique, which could span at least two realities; for example, the abrupt changes of focus throughout "Christmas Eve," where a witch and the devil explicitly participate. Yet he found additional ways to promote what Frank calls "simultaneity of perception" within the medium of language, which necessarily proceeds in time.[9] While fashioning the present, Gogol often kept one eye upon the future. The result is a present which cannot quite completely conceal what follows. In this sense, early appearances serve as the background paper which the future slowly, eerily develops. As we perceive them, later events therefore seem faintly familiar.

The primary devices Gogol used for achieving this effect are ironic foreshadowings, prophetic irony, and forward-leaning (or "interlocking") details. Forward-leaning details could also be termed ironic foreshadowings, except that they often seem so completely insignificant in context. Later, however, when such a detail subtly "interlocks" with another, the reader becomes uneasily aware of a faint pattern connecting apparently unrelated and unimportant elements. In retrospect, the first detail acquires a tinge of anticipation. With effects of "prophetic irony," certain words seem (in retrospect only) to have explicitly, though perhaps unwittingly, applied to the future. Both Thomas Hardy and Vladimir Nabokov also greatly favor this technique.

Gogol's fondness for "interlocking detail" often results in pairs of strikingly similar images. These may be adjacent or very far apart. Sometimes, such pairs seem to reinforce, even to modify, a third image. They may thus be called "descriptive double images." The device occurs most frequently in *Dead Souls.*

Other chronological techniques include an ending essential to explain what precedes it ("The Terrible Vengeance," "The Portrait") and an ending which tends to project itself into the future ("Shponka," *The Government Inspector*). Still another is the use of titles that expand in meaning as the work develops ("The Terrible Vengeance," *The Government Inspector*). In addition, Gogol occasionally merges narrative (the reader's) and fable (the story's) time,[10] but not without ironic twists (*Dead Souls,* "May Night . . ."). On a smaller scale, syllogistic narration and the haunting return (in digressions) also contribute to a feeling that the future has been folded back over the present.

Syllogistic narration comprises a three-part presentation of two antinomic extremes, uneasily reconciled. (Sobakevich seems to have no soul, or if he did have a soul, it was hidden away so deep that no ripple remained on the surface. Thus, we have: (1) no soul, (2) a soul, and (3) no effective soul.) The device may be said to take the reader back to where he started, only to realize that he is now somewhere else.[11] Somewhat similarly, Gogolian "digressions" often subtly return almost to their point of departure in what may be called a "haunting return." (The silent, inquisitive cockroaches in Chichikov's hotel room are soon followed, in context, by a silent, inquisitive neighbor.) Conversely (and much less often), a "focusing in" abruptly becomes a "focusing out." (The man who appears on the first page of *Dead Souls,* described all the way down to the shape of his tiepin, soon vanishes forever.)

As in a sudden cinematic close-up, Gogolian focus frequently catches a scene which long remains with the reader. We still see Manilov and his gaping mouth,[12] Shponka finally speaking up about the multitude of flies in summer, the paralyzed finale of *The Government Inspector,* the uncanny twilight whereby both Ivans (one naked, one clothed) argue, Akaky's beclouded reaction to the

ominous declaration that he must have a new overcoat. Gogol, we
could say, freezes time. Certain pictures, certain scenes, remain with
us as we view others. Background legends and stories (of vengeance,
or drowned maidens, of Viy, of the devil disguised as a pig and
seeking fragments of his red jacket) show through and color the
present. Yet more: this twofold focus holds true even for episodes
within the story proper, adding a tinge of eerie expectation. One
scene typically continues, or develops, behind another. Established
early, suggestions of the Government Inspector "on his way" linger
throughout the entire play; the General and his officers ride inexorably on to visit Chertokutsky and his carriage, while their host lies
oblivious in bed and his wife dallies blissfully before the mirror;
Pirogov smugly follows his blonde while we read a long digression
about the society to which he belonged. (The effect is slightly twisted
with Manilov and Chichikov in *Dead Souls* and Kalenik in "Christmas Eve.")

Just as Gogolian reverse vision enabled the future to show
through the present, so it promoted a shining of evil (emanating
perhaps from another world or reality) through goodness and
beauty. Despite man's lofty aspirations and capacity for delicate
feelings, he is often seen as an animal who hides his body in rather
ridiculously important clothes. In fact, the clothes frequently seem
almost more alive than the person inside. Gogol's faintly alien perspective, we could say, simply does not recognize normal bound-
aries. Almost as if seen by a being from another planet, our clothes
and bodies seem to merge.[13] Heads are strangely featured as ideas
occur to them. Ideas, one comes to feel, have—are—a separate reality. They even seem to exist both inside and outside the human
head.[14]

In Gogol's world, man's body is seen in a most uneasy light.
Functioning naturally, the human body reverses delicious, sweet-
smelling food. The body's appetites are self-consciously tinged with
a faint repulsiveness. Food suggests flies and garbage; kissing suggests smoking; drinking and dancing are seen as rather numb, mechanical rituals; sex is closely associated with food, perhaps as two
appetites, both of which uneasily involve both ends of the body.[15]
All this uneasiness also attends normal human relationships. Fathers
are strangely drawn to their daughters. Women are constantly

mentioned alongside the devil. Even the most beautiful women seem to have an almost evil glow. Their bodies shine deceptively, like cold statues made of ghostly marble.[16] Amorous advances are often interrupted.

Life itself seems a rather uneasy condition. And if writers may be said to focus upon a fear of death (for example, Tolstoy), then perhaps Gogol may be said (not without exaggeration, of course) to suggest a fear of life—at least in its normal conscious condition. For in Gogol's world, it seems that normal conscious perception may well be an insidiously self-sufficient deception, from which the only relief, or escape, is death (Akaky finally "releases" his ghostly soul).

In sum, Gogol's vision often tended to reverse good and bad, life and death, the real and the unreal, day and night, God and the devil, reflections (in water, mirrors) and what is reflected, laughter and tears.

Gogol is famous for his "sad laughter" or "laughter through tears." These labels ostensibly derive from the following pronouncement in *Dead Souls:*

> And a supernatural power has ordained that for a long time yet I must walk hand in hand with my strange heroes, must view all of life as it rushes hugely along, view it through laughter the world sees and through tears the world sees not and knows not. (VI:134)

What is Gogol really saying here? First, he has subtly exchanged the "reality" of his heroes with that of life. With reverse vision, Gogol sees himself as a companion of his (fictitious) heroes, viewing the movielike panorama of ("real") life as it rushes hugely by. Second, he feels compelled to see life itself with the world's reaction (laughter) and, in addition, with his own reverse one (tears). The statement thus seems a double claim to, or admission of, reverse vision. And perhaps it is not, as commonly thought,[17] so much a description of the general effect of Gogol's writing as an insight into his own creative vision. Yet there is surely considerable justification for supposing an atmosphere of "sad humor" about Gogol's world.

Goglian humor often turns on ironic reversals. In "Sorochintsy," for example, the words "apparently unintentionally" suggest a very purposeful display of breasts. These breasts, moreover, are by inference an "offering" for a priest's son. And in "Christmas Eve," the word "honor" serves to describe a woman's efficiency in satisfying, separately, her numerous lovers.

A third product of reverse vision (and Gogol's most eerie effect) is that another world seems to keep showing through, overlapping, even breaking into, this one. Conversely, dreams may contain a "terrifying fragment of reality." Dreams are often prophetic.[18] The imaginary, the fantastic, the supernatural, are strangely vivid and perhaps more real than the furnishings of our supposedly firm, solid world. Insanity is presented as almost disturbingly logical. The unreal is matter-of-factly presumed to be part of reality.

All this relates to the general Gogolian theme of deceptive appearances, which, stylistically, is relentlessly promoted by the device of false focus. Most often, Gogol employs false focus to refer to someone already dead, or who has altered greatly in appearance, or who is really someone (or something) else. "The deceased" named her son "Akaky Akakevich"; "one samovar" has a beard; "Katherine's father" is really the sorcerer; "the Government Inspector" is not the Government Inspector, and so on. The effect of this device is to call our attention to a deceptively multiple reality. ("The Enchanted Place" seems to be two places.) Our perception, as we realize that one reference signifies at least two, literally expands. We are left with a lingering suspicion that far more of our world is deceptive. And the effect seems perversely vivid. Not unlike negative psychology, false focus is surprisingly persuasive. Realizing that an appearance is deceptive, the reader strains to picture, simultaneously, an overlapping of realities. Thus, Gogolian false focus involves not merely a dual identity, but the (strangely vivid) perception-expanding use of one label to evoke both identitites at once.[19] In what may be considered a variation of this device, Gogol describes something by denying two opposites ("neither . . . nor") and then gradually focuses in upon one of them.

Besides relentless false focus, two other elements in Gogolian narration promote the effect of deceptive appearances: alien, or eerie, frames of reference and unseen backgrounds. The first presents unsettling insights into a sinister "reality" behind our own. For example: "The devil, it could be seen (vidno), led him to kiss her."

Or: In hell, "as is well known" *(kak izvestno)*, it is terribly hot. Second, Gogol often features an unseen audience in scenes already described to the reader. We suddenly discover that the kissing we were observing was also being watched by someone else, who has been standing in the doorway for some time. While we were being introduced to a character, another was also present, and so on. Such "live backgrounds" tend to include the reader, to make him feel that he is but one of several spectators within the story itself. (A somewhat similar effect results from Gogol's tendency to describe a situation as suddenly "more" something than it was—when the "was" has never been mentioned. Plyushkin is suddenly "more suspicious"; the mystic signs of the sorcerer's wall suddenly begin changing "more rapidly.") Still another technique exploits the very common Russian word *uzhe* ("already") to make people vanish before we realize it. With rather strange symmetry, then, Gogolian people often appear (as unseen backgrounds) and disappear (by means of the "already" device) before the reader is fully aware of it. We thus have the sensation of having blinked our eyes and missed something: the action is vividly compressed.

Gogol used the flexibility of word order in Russian to enhance various effects. In a technique which may be termed broken description, words are inserted (and usually set off by commas) between, say, adjective and noun or verb and direct object. For instance: "her bright, like lightening, eyes" or "he uttered, like the devil himself, a terrible oath." (Obviously, these effects are frequently erased in translation.) At such times, Gogol is often otherwise suggesting the overlapping of two realities within the story. Thus the choppy, broken word order may be seen to reinforce the notion of one world briefly showing through another.[20] Quite literally, the lightning and devil "show through" the eyes and oath. As noted above, both Zenkovsky and Nabokov have stressed the unexpected "breaking through" in Gogol's style of material from what seems to be another world.

However, it cannot be overemphasized that such broken arrangements of wording are far more natural in Russian than in English. (Proffer has cautiously observed that in a Russian sentence which translates "Words, like hawks, flew out"—the vehicle "seems to split the tenor. Does "hawks" modify "words" or "flew out"? [21]) The examples noted in the present study mostly involve insertions between an adjective and its noun. And though such broken wordings are quite natural in Russian, they often attend, and perhaps enhance, in Gogol's world, a brief break in the seemingly solid surface of reality. The technique may be seen as related, on a smaller scale, to the abrupt shift of focus noted above between various scenes or realities within a given work.

Gogol frequently inserted the words "even" *(dazhe)* and "almost" *(pochti)* in such a way "as to make the harmless sentence explode in a wild display of nightmare fireworks," as Nabokov has phrased it.[22] Gogolian uses of the word "even" have been described by Dmitry Chizhevsky.[23] "Almost" is often joined with "always" *(vsegda)* or "never *(nikogda)* for an uneasy or unsettling effect. (In "Old World Landowners," Afanasy "almost never" (II:16) recalled his past life as an officer, which is paralled by apparently casual descriptions in the "present" of the story.)

Gogol also played upon shades of meaning in certain Russian words for both humorous and eerie effect. *Neobyknovennyj* ("unusual") often hints at the supernatural, so that it becomes a sly, ironic understatement. Two other favorites are *verno* and *vidno (vid,* "aspect," is very often used in deceptive appearances). These words often promote uncanny or unwitting insights. Their colloquial meanings *(verno,* "probably"; *vidno,* "apparently") are often employed when their more literal meanings ("surely" or "truly" and "it can be seen") seem rather unsettling. This tends to enhance eerie frames of reference: She was "surely" in league with the devil; This, "it could be seen," was the devil's work. Similarly, the word *kazhetsya* ("it seems") often raises the uneasy question: To whom? We may also note an occasional Gogolian reversal of what "is known" *(izvestno)* to the narrator and what "is not known." For example, it is "not known" what happened to a barber on a bridge (III:52), but it "is known" that the devil was alone with, and making amorous advances to, a witch (I:217). *Verit'* ("to trust," "to believe") is often ominously negated. *Natural'no* ("naturally") often becomes ironic if taken literally ("by nature"). Especially in the "Ivans" tale, Gogol plays upon the phrases "in this world" *(na ètom svete)* and "in the next world" *(na tom svete).* Eerie effects sometimes result from phrases like "in all directions" and "from all sides." The negative particle *ne* often contributes to sly ironies.

Generally, Gogolian vision tended to reverse the degree of effectiveness in verbal communication. People speak many words but say little, yet "the unsaid" is often vividly evocative. Rumor is often more powerful than truth. Purposeful redundancy sometimes parallels a slowly dawning idea. In short, the Word is persistently viewed as a capricious and unreliable, yet strangely magical entity.[24]

I. A. Richards has referred to words in a poem as having "very definite senses in delicate interaction" with those of the other words.[25] Yuri Tynyanov has suggested that in context, a word is "a chameleon." [26] Gogol's use of "interlocking detail" enabled him to give the impression of digressing without entirely leaving a given subject, situation, or idea. When separate, but similar, details occur in a single passage, they often seem united by an alien, yet oddly consistent point of view.[27] Narrational focus moves from one point to another in an erratic, yet strangely harmonious, path. Examples of this may be found in the "champagne glass" digression ("Nevsky Prospect"), the "vinegar bottle" digression ("The Portrait"), and the sly anticipations of rain in *Dead Souls*.

Similarly, Gogolian precarious logic seems alien but often disturbingly plausible. The technique is disarming because, as in dreams, normal cause-and-effect relationships are matter-of-factly distorted, yet the whole nevertheless remains structured, so that one tends not to question the connections involved. Nabokov's term "irrational insight" [28] comes to mind.

The effects of "precarious logic" range from playful humor to an undermining of reality itself. A man's face resembles a sheep's because, when his mother was giving birth, a sheep bleated in at the window. The word "millionaire" is humorously blamed for qualities discerned in Chichikov. But such humor, in Gogol's world, can turn almost deadly serious. With a faintly eerie persistence, human heads are focused in conjunction with the birth of ideas. What is apparently "a most insignificant occurrence" can lead to an entire sequence of strangely related events (as in "The Overcoat") or even to death (as in "Old World Landowners"). People seem humorously helpless to discern the patterns in their lives. Even their own tongues often fail to obey them. And when words are uttered as intended, a casual oath about the devil will frequently seem to confirm, or even inspire, the devil's interference in the speaker's life. Rather than ruled by fate, man seems placed in a strange arena to do battle with alien forces, some playful, some lethal, and many invisible.

Dostoevsky's Underground Man insists that consciousness is a disease. In Kierkegaard's view, our desire to prolong our present state of existence resembles a sick man's desire for precisely that which feeds his affliction. Nabokov's writing has moved one critic to speculate: "the assumption that a human being lives in and can apprehend a comfortable 'factual' reality is the most disturbing parody of all." [29] Gogol's writing gently but persistently promotes the suspicion that our consciousness—our awareness of reality—is an insidiously soothing deception.[30] By combining a faintly alien point of view with faintly alien presumptions about what is viewed, Gogol's writing tends to expand the reader's consciousness. Especially the effects of reverse vision, false focus, and precarious logic generate and sustain this expansion, until we feel, as Bely suggests, that Gogol's art is wretchedly narrowed by our own perceptual faculties. In Gogol's world, we suspect that even during moments of heightened consciousness, Something eludes or evades us. The ultimate effect is of glimpses into a region both alien and strangely familiar, even kindred, which we *almost* perceive in our normal conscious state but which, perhaps, is a dimension more familiar to the human soul.[31]

Notes

1. In her introduction to Belyj's *Lug zelyonyj,* Zoya Yur'eva offers and discusses some reasons for this return (pp. xxi-xxv).

2. Gogol thanked God for giving him the strength to burn his drafts of Part Two of *Dead Souls* in 1845; he blamed the final burning, in 1852, on the devil's powerful inspiration. See Carl R. Proffer, ed., *Letters of Nikolai Gogol* (Ann Arbor, 1967), pp. 13-14, 20.

3. Nabokov, p. 142.

4. Muchnic, p. 23.

5. See Nabokov, p. 32.

6. As I have tried to show in this study, Gogol's earlier works contain many of the same basic ingredients as his better, mature ones.

7. Muchnic, pp. 28-29.

8. Joseph Frank, "Spatial Form in Modern Literature," in *Critiques and Essays in Criticism: 1920-1948,* Robert Wooster Stallman, ed. (New York, 1949), p. 322.

9. This assertion of Frank's could be debated. For example, John Barth has written parallel columns of print intended to be read simultaneously (*The Floating Opera,* New York, 1967; pp. 172-74). A similar effect could be obtained by reading while listening to a (calculated supplementary) recorded voice. Still, even such dual perceptions must "proceed in time," and they may be considered (in the sense, say, that one cannot see an optical illusion in two different ways at exactly the same time) merely as an extreme example of the focus shifting Frank has noted in Flaubert.

10. See René Wellek and Austin Warren, *Theory of Literature* (New York, 1956), p. 208.

11. See my "Gogolesque Perception-Expanding Reversals in Nabokov," p. 118.

12. Perhaps because of the prominence of noses in Gogol's works, the importance of mouths seems yet to be fully acknowledged.

13. It has been said that clothing is not the antithesis of nakedness but its accomplice. In *Dead Souls,* the women of town N wear party dresses which, we read, "concealed in front and in back that which could not bring about a man's ruin, yet they forced one to suspect that precisely there was his very ruin" (VI:163). And in the short fragment "A Street Lamp Was Dying . . ." we are told that "a woman in a white dress" can cause one's feelings to become concentrated in the fragrance of the dress and in the barely audible, musical sound it produces. "This is the very highest and most voluptuous voluptuousness [*sic*]." (III:330-31).

14. In Part Two of *Dead Souls,* Chichikov reflects that it may be possible to avoid repaying the money he has borrowed from Kostanzhoglo: "A strange thought, it was not as if Chichikov had it, but it suddenly, all on its own, appeared, teasing, smirking, and winking at him" (VII:89).

15. It has been said that one can learn about how a person makes love by watching him eat.

Gogol's tendency to view food and the human body as faintly repulsive and disgusting surfaces rather vividly in "Viy" during a description of the seminarists in class. After eating melons, they produced "two lessons: one issued from their lips, the other rumbled in their senatorial stomachs" (II:157).

16. During the nocturnal riding scene in "Viy," Homa seems a water

nymph, whose "cloudlike" breasts shine like "porcelain," illuminated "along the edges of their white, elastically-soft roundness" (II:186).

17. Misquotations of the original, such as the one in Aleksandr Slonimskij, p. 9, which omits the basic reversal, are unfortunate.

18. Leonard J. Kent, in *The Subconscious in Gogol' and Dostoevskij, and Its Antecedents* (The Hague, 1969), has noted the "anticipatory" function of Katherine's dream in "The TerribleVengeance" (that her father will kill her) and of Chartkov's dream (of the coins) in "The Portrait" (pp. 66, 83). He concludes that with Gogol "the dream and other manifestations of the subconscious" reflect backward, project ahead, and reflect inward (p. 86).

19. Coming from a Ukrainian writing in Italy, phrases like *"u nas na Rusi"* ("here in Russia" or "in our Russia," VI:49) seem especially ironic in their false focus.

20. Yu. V. Mann (p. 227) quotes Gogol's description of the gypsy (who helps Grytsko) in "The Sorochintsy Fair," italicizing a broken description: "live, like fire, eyes." He then terms the description "dualistic"—a portrait of a common vagabond containing, however, features of the strange person who usually appeared as the personified incarnation of an evil force. N. L. Stepanov, who finds that the uniqueness of Gogol's Romanticism lies in its close ties with folklore and folk poetry (p. 198), suggests that Gogolian lyrical digressions help to create a Romantic effect of dual realities (pp. 214, 218). Stepanov quotes, but does not discuss as such, a broken description in "The Diary of a Madman" where two realities seem to overlap (see note 3 to that story, above).

21. Proffer, *Simile,* p. 33.

22. Nabokov, p. 142.

23. Dmitrij Chizhevskij, "O 'Shineli' Gogolya," pp. 173-74, 178-84.

24. In a four-page article entitled "On What the Word is," Gogol argues that since a writer's words are his deeds, he must avoid using them dishonestly, much as a judge must avoid taking bribes. In Russian, *slovom* ("in a word") can also mean "by means of the word." Gogol goes on to say that a man who uses words carelessly can be harmful to himself: "In a word [or: by means of the word], he slanders himself at every turn. It is dangerous for a writer to joke with the word" (VIII:232). Of six such lone uses of *slovom,* five may be seen, in varying shades, to be unwittingly playful. And in these same four pages, Gogol solemnly declares that Derzhavin hurt himself very much by not burning at least half of his odes (230). Two sentences later, we learn more precisely what should have been burned: those places not filled with "an inner force of spiritual fire."

25. I. A. Richards, "The Bridle of Pegasus," *Critiques and Essays . . . ,* p. 299.

26. Yurij Tynyanov, *Problema stikhotvornogo yazyka* (Moscow, 1965), p. 77.

27. Gogol has been reproached by I. E. Mandel'shtam (*O kharaktere gogolevskogo stilya;* St. Petersburg, 1902; pp. 75-76) for digressing so that the reader forgets about the point of departure (in likening the males to flies and the females to lumps of sugar at a party early in *Dead Souls,* VI:14). Proffer has questioned the accuracy of this charge (p. 69). Nabokov has noted that the passage contains a verbal pattern that forms "a complete circle" (p. 79). Moreover, so many details about the flies and sugar seem to echo and describe the men and women (for example, the males' winglike frock coats, their ostentatious back-and-forth motions, the rubbing and scratching of their legs) that contrary to obscuring the party scene, Gogol's digression develops and even brightens with rather uneasy insights the picture from which his narration has apparently swerved away.

28. Nabokov, p. 140.

29. Dabney Stuart, "*Laughter in the Dark:* dimensions of parody," in *Nabokov,* Appel and Newman, eds. (Evanston, Ill., 1970), p. 94.

30. Stuart also finds (p. 93) that Nabokov's novel implies that "human perception is inevitably imaginative." Nabokov himself has suggested that "imagination is a form of memory." The circle seems uneasily complete. Like figures in a painting, we cannot raise our heads and look about. But Gogol's writing makes us aware of the painting.

31. As Nabokov has put it, Gogol's writing "appeals to that secret depth of the human soul where the shadows of other worlds pass like the shadows of nameless and soundless ships" (p. 149).

Index

199